DESIGN STUDIO
2023 VOLUME 7

Design Studio Vol. 7 Full Spectrum – Colour in Contemporary Architecture is printed on White Offset 300gsm and White Offset 120gsm paper, FSC®. Papers Carbon Balanced by the World Land Trust. Printed with eco-friendly high-quality vegetable-based inks by Pureprint Group, the world's first carbon neutral printer.

Published by RIBA Publishing,
66 Portland Place, London, W1B 1AD

ISBN 978 1 915722 03 4

British Library Cataloguing-in-Publication Data

A catalogue record for this book is available from the British Library.

Commissioning Editor: Alex White
Assistant Editor: Clare Holloway
Production: Marie Doinne
Designed and typeset by Linda Byrne
Printed and bound by Pureprint Group Ltd
Cover design: Linda Byrne

www.ribapublishing.com

DESIGN STUDIO 2023 VOLUME 7

ARTICLES

PROFILES

CASE STUDIES

About the Editors

Elena Manferdini is the principal and owner of Atelier Manferdini in Los Angeles and Graduate Programs Chair at Southern California Institute of Architecture (SCI-Arc). With a body of work that spans public art, architecture and industrial design, her eponymous Atelier has created work on three continents that uplifts the human spirit. Her design is known for its vibrant colours, meaningful narratives and its high attention to novel materials and craft. Elena Manferdini has more than 20 years of professional experience and she is a leading voice in contemporary design culture and education. In 2019, Manferdini was honoured with the ICON Award as part of the LA Design Festival, which is a prize that recognises iconic women who have made an indelible mark on Los Angeles, culture and society in general through their work, character and creative leadership.

Jasmine Benyamin is a historian, theorist and critic with more than 25 years of combined professional and academic experience. She was previously Associate Professor of Architecture at the University of Wisconsin – Milwaukee School of Architecture and Urban Planning and currently serves as lecturer at the University of Southern California (USC) School of Architecture. A recipient of numerous awards, her recent interdisciplinary research addresses architectural manifestations in art practice and popular culture, with a particular focus on film and photography. She holds Bachelor's degrees in architecture and French literature from Columbia University, a Master of Architecture degree from Yale University and a PhD from Princeton University. In addition to editing and translating several books on architecture, her essays and reviews have appeared in numerous scholarly journals and anthologies. Her book, entitled *MASTERcrit*, was published in 2022 with ORO Editions.

Full Spectrum

Colour in Contemporary Architecture

Editors' Introduction

Elena Manferdini and Jasmine Benyamin

Sauerbruch Hutton, Brandhorst Museum
with Tuerkentor in the rear, Munich, 2009.

The importance of colour in the world... surpasses any limits yet conceived.[1]
Fernand Léger

From the polychromy of the ancients to the great white interiors of high modernism, from the figurative flourishes of postmodernism to the embedded intelligence of contemporary building systems and facades, colour has played a central role in the history of architecture. Straddling objective truths and subjective tastes, colour has indexed all manner of values: beauty, femininity and virility, but also vulgarity, queerness and primitivity. At best, colour is God-given and at worst a distraction. To be sure, as Carolyn Kane's discussion of Le Corbusier's Law of Ripolin reminds us, whitewashing has largely been driven by Western European myths of purity and universalism, resulting in acute bouts of chromophobia; ironic, given that the study of colour theory was required alongside foundation courses at the Bauhaus. Indeed, the story and history of this monotone (read: white) approach is more complicated and nuanced.

This volume of *Design Studio* is one attempt at expanding current storylines on colour. The compiled essays, profiles and case studies are emphatically not comprehensive. Rather, they drop anchors on specific moments where architecture and colour engage important topics. New and established voices have been invited to share their perspectives, in the hope of presenting a wide spectrum of avenues for thinking and making.

The answers have been both reassuring and surprising, at times upending our own preconceptions about the topic. Particularly within the context of contemporary spatial practices, certain themes have emerged – some more anticipated than others. Perhaps most importantly, they all confirmed our core belief: colour today is architecture's sharpest tool in the box. In fact, it has experienced a renaissance: as the field of authors and producers in and around the profession has rightly broadened to include a rich constellation of vantage points, colour has become a mode of working, a cultural provocation and a political proposition. This is true of those practices that align themselves with emerging technologies, but also of other work that we believe bears equal weight in current architectural discourse.

All have a stake in the expanded field of colour and architecture.

The promise and perils of digital colour

In recent years we have witnessed an exponential growth of digital colour applications. New equipment and visualisation techniques have expanded our vision into a full spectrum of potentialities. Digital screens have become pervasive, beaming light into the eyes of the beholders, while the intersection of coloured light with human vision has entered a new normal. As a consequence, our chromatic thinking has entered previously uncharted territories. Galo Canizares' and Maya Alam's contributions expand on chromatic techniques and mapping tools available today.

Alam's essay explores the topic, particularly the ways in which emergent technologies have inherent

Maya Alam, 'Casa Zwei', 2018–.

Freddy Mamani Silvestre, Salón de fiestas 'Diamante', Ciudad de El Alto, Bolivia, 2017.

biases – biases that mirror prejudices in contemporary society, which too often dictate standards of beauty. She draws parallels with female-led practices, whose applications of colour in their projects serve as sites of protest. While leveraging colourised point cloud[2] scanning, their work flickers between creative 'now-ness' and resistance; rarely seen back-of-house glitches visualise a combination of textures and patterns that remain unaltered. These digital gaps enable multivalent narratives of resistance that target prevailing norms and gender roles.

Canizares insists that a fuller apprehension of digital colour requires a certain degree of technical expertise, alongside an appreciation for its representative and interpretive powers. His interest lies not only in those design firms whose 'expanded consciousness of colour' deploy chroma techniques, but also in other projects that analogise virtual space by mimicking default physical properties.

Marcelyn Gow's essay focuses on the role that education has in propelling chromatic possibilities. Her text analyses three installations that took place at the Southern California Institute for Architecture (SCI-Arc), in Los Angeles. The school is well known for being at the forefront of the digital revolution and for its exuberant digital visualisations. These installations are examples of the spectrum of possibilities that architectural colour can hold when applied to creative forms of teaching. Conceived as a collaboration between faculties and students, the white box gallery becomes a place where digital colours leave the monitors and project themselves in real life.

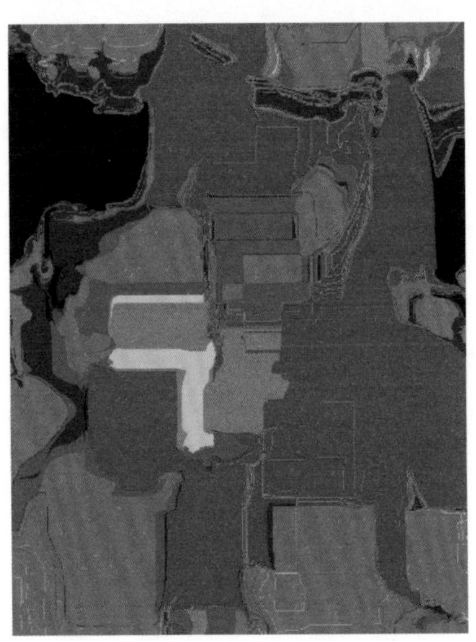

Galo Canizares, *THREADS – 211017-01_107*, 2022.

Guto Requena interacting with WZ Hotel Jardins' 'Light Creature' installation, São Paulo, 2015.

Colour's new sites and audiences

As Courtney Coffman notes, architectural thinking where colour is concerned simultaneously contends with questions of objectivity and subjectivity. Her deep dive into the work of Bolivian architect Freddy Mamani Silvestre illustrates the ways in which colour is utilised as a cultural (in his case Indigenous Andean) index of regional identity: in a world of digital alternatives, colour has the unique capacity to mobilise 'our identity and communicate our self-prescribed ideologies'.

Guto Requena's and Amanda Williams' practices tell stories on behalf of the voiceless. Their engagements with colour reflect a commitment to their respective (often overlooked) communities. Both used social media to democratise the reach of their work, harnessing it to great effect. Williams' turn to Instagram during the pandemic was partly borne out of necessity. What began as a commentary on racism and police violence grew into a months-long series of tonal blacks thickened by extended captions addressing a singular prompt: which black?

Many of Requena's projects strive to highlight and uplift the LGBTQ+ community in Brazil. His high-rise installation entitled 'Light Creature' capitalises on the ubiquity of handheld mobile devices in two ways: in the first instance and using a mobile app, passers-by interact with the installation through touch and sound. In the second instance, photographs and videos of the kinetic light show are posted online, proliferating on shared platforms. Both Requena and Williams effectively leverage the hegemony of Instagram and its viral cult for hedonistic visuals to build spaces for new stakeholders. If architecture has become a background to the lives we share online, then its colours can carry messages accessible to broader constituencies. Colour holds the potential to define identity, amplifying both differences and commonalities.

Above and previous page: 100architects, 'Over the Rainbow', Changsha, China, 2021.

The chromatic city

Colour's popularity – alongside both its associative possibilities and communicative properties – provides fertile ground for more heterogeneous connections with the public. Employing the full range of colour puts forth a mode of action whose stance is both critical and projective. It aids the democratisation of visual culture, opening the field to enable new subjectivities, references and points of view.

100architects' embrace of colour and social media manifests at the scale of the city, whereby the urban realm has come to serve as backdrop to our selfies. The feedback loop in their practice does not rely on academia or fine art institutions, but rather on the viral 'likes' and spontaneous responses of residents and tourists. This mass audience demands photogenic settings, which in turn inform the production of richly pigmented installations. 100architects' playscapes do not operate solely as local and temporal experiences, but as shared, highly filtered posts that anyone can view and like. Their footprints reside in our mobile phone feeds more than in our physical experience.

Sauerbruch Hutton, M9 Museum District, Venice-Mestre, 2018.

Sauerbruch Hutton also explore the vital role that colour plays as an urban signifier. The firm excels in civic buildings whose tectonic extroversion pays homage to Gottfried Semper's exploration of textiles. Often intervening in historic city centres, their seemingly pixelated enclosures deploy colour as a thread that stitches austere volumes with their surroundings. Perceptually distinct up close as they are at a distance, their buildings are best engaged while on the move. David Batchelor's artworks and installations distil this vantage point on colour in the city by setting their sights on luminosity. Luminescent colour is temporal and, as such, fragile and futile. Neon, fluorescent and LEDs produce unnatural colours. At a perceptual level, their effectiveness increases as day approaches night. Widely available and off the shelf, these ubiquitous colours arguably perform best when scaled up.

Not just surface effects

Louisa Hutton's assertion of architecture's 'both-and' capacity to use colour extends to other practitioners in the volume. Sam Jacob's work, too, questions colour's often-maligned status as (merely) surface application. While the priority of the work is not to frontload nascent drawing techniques, its chromatic approach is contemporary and culturally contextual. In all cases, its flat application coincides with a simultaneous perception of depth. At the urban scale, the intentionally alien colour palettes render contemporary otherwise familiar historical surroundings. fala's approach to colour is similarly site driven: their houses in Portugal reflect local vernacular building traditions, while their modest material applications and restrained formal vocabulary (fittingly represented in collage) belie the complexity of their outcomes: spatial compositions that use novel hue palettes as foils between two and three dimensions.

Sam Jacob Studio, Kingly Court, London, 2018.

fala, 067, 2018.

Conclusion

If the following pages illustrate a wealth of enthusiastic responses to colour, Paulette Singley offers a cautionary tale. Her essay paints a picture that depicts the perils of 'greenwashing' – a trap in which architects have been known to fall. It is not a novelty to describe the discipline of architecture as one which borrows from others, yet nowhere is this trap more evident than in the realm of sustainability. Too often, 'green architecture' has been flattened to a rhetorical gesture; 'green' is both the subject and object of myriad narratives signifying all manner of eco resilience when, in the best scenarios, a better word for it might very well be 'regeneration'.

Nevertheless, we remain optimistic. Today, colour in architecture is imaginative, multivalent and speculative. Colour provides the binding agent between individual identities and a collective unconscious. Whether discussed historically as a disciplinary outlier, or as a dynamic time-based medium, as a vehicle to explore discrimination or as both a situated material and technical instrument, colour charts new maps for engagement with the built environment. In short, it is everywhere.

1 Léger F, 'Problèmes de la Couleur', 1954, in *Functions of Painting*, New York: Viking Press, 1973, p 188.
2 A point cloud, typically created using laser scanning or photogrammetry, is a set of data representing the external 3D shape of a real-world object or scene using many individual dots in a 3D space. Each dot contains information about its position and colour, creating a digital copy.

Arch-White

Carolyn Kane

Ripolin advertisement in the Australian magazine *Building* Vol 3, No 23-12, July 1909. A 'ready to use' paint with a 'porcelain'-like finish, the commercial brand of ready-mixed paints boasted an impermeable and washable enamel, free from the colours of dirt and disease.

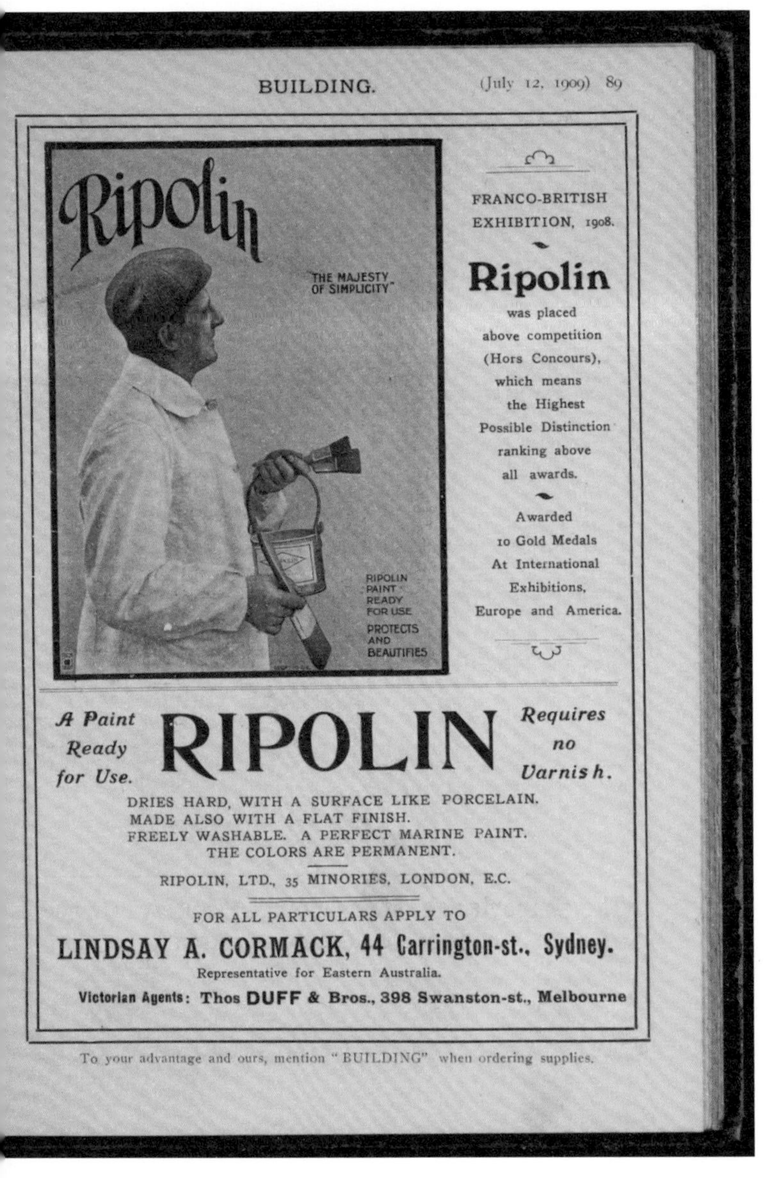

The White House

Whiteness imparts infinite contradictions. In the global northwest, whiteness has for centuries claimed exclusive right to transcendental knowledge, moral superiority and universal objectivity ('He judges not merely for himself, but for everyone,'[1] as Kant put it in 1790) and yet, whiteness only exists as a synthetic effect of historical construction, detached from any particular person, place or thing. As one fresh coat of whitewash is painted on top of another, each new layer appears natural and true, erasing awareness of the colourful sediment that came before it. Granted, whiteness offers only the most egregious account of racism in the West, and in the history of architecture in particular; it is nonetheless here that we begin, only to move backwards in time to illustrate how the links between whiteness and architecture not only remain with us today, but do so as the most ancient of racial encodings. Put differently, recent scholarship has begun to show the racial underpinnings of Euro-American architecture through a constant return to its long history of false and misguided reinterpretations. Without whitewashing away the politics of these efforts, this essay aims to return here, once again, to illustrate how the many colours obscured in the history of architectural white can be remade for architects today.

Contrary to conventional scholarly accounts that fasten whiteness to Euro-American legacies, whiteness must instead be understood as belonging to a multitude of cultures, as old as civilisation itself.[2] From approximately 10,000 to 4,500 BC, a 4,000-year transition arose in the Near East, from the Stone Age's nomadic tribes of hunter-gathers into a Neolithic period of foragers residing in semi-subterranean mud-lined oval spaces, into settler-based agriculture communities with permanent enclosures.[3] Mark Wigley suggests the latter, proto-architectural shelters, inaugurated the first civilisational ordering system that simultaneously formed itself into an unanticipated incubator for new forms of disease and illnesses which, in turn, required ritual cleaning and cleansing. The archetypical white house was herein born. In effect, a human-made petri dish for engineering and depositing pathogens. As a result of these 'inter-species intimacies', humans grew collectively weaker (the introduction of mass tuberculosis infection during this time, for instance, led to a collapse of the human spine and an overall decline in human health).[4]

Early settler communities responded to the influx of disease by developing techniques to clean and purify the house, to sanitise it of dirt and disease and, hence, whitewashing was born – *in the East*, that is, through the work and ingenuity of people of colour – as a means of ensuring human, plant and animal survival. It 'is not that architecture was whitened', Wigley writes, but it is 'only architecture inasmuch as it [is] white'.[5] The skin of a body that houses a people and the skin of a people that protect it are both, in the end, one and the same: weak and permeable membranes fluctuating between inside and outside, dependent on the perpetual innovation of new coats of whitewash technologies for longevity and prosperity.

Whiteness as possession

Whitewashing only became a problem of race and ethnicity when such cleansing practices were appropriated as a form of possession; a property claimed by one group and used as a weapon of exclusion, oppression and control. One such early inroad is found in Greek physician Hippocrates' (460–370 BC) 'Airs, waters, places' (400 BC), which articulates a form of proto-racial profiling linking northern, southern, western and eastern cultures to illness. Hippocrates' text is far from the full-fledged racial profiling that marks dark-skinned bodies as antithetical to white ones today, but it is an ur-theory[6] of skin colour as indicator of health and intrinsic merit. If bodies are awash in too much colour, he appealed, whether this be whiteness or darkness, the health and ecosystem are threatened. 'Good' health fell in the middle zone, in a colour balance between light and dark.[7]

In his 'On colours', Greek philosopher Aristotle likewise argued that colours inhering in an object indicated relative health. When a plant reached its most intense state of green, a flower its most intense hue or a so-called 'white' person the most pink, it indicated a being flourishing at the height of its life force.[8] Unlike Hippocrates, for Aristotle these changes marked a natural part of an object's life cycle, not a proto-theory of racial hierarchy. Either way, these two colour theories offer examples of a unique dismantling of problematic links between skin colour and race or ethnicity, while simultaneously revealing the ways in which the surface colour of the skin has, since the origins of civilisation, played a pivotal role signifying health and wealth, which is to say, power and privilege.

As societies evolved, so did the whitewashing materials used to build, protect and sanitise it. With each evolution, the whiteness of white architecture took on the veneer of the radically new and, at times, revolutionary. This is because architecture *must* forge itself as original, a firstness denoted in the prefix 'arch', deriving from the Greek ἄρχω *(arkhi)*, meaning chief, beginning or leading or, in Proto-Indo-European, meaning to begin, rule or command. If whiteness is always first, then arch is always white. In turn, *techné* derives from the Greek τέχνη (tékhne) and denotes a technology of making or building. In essence, to build an origin, *after the fact* (nothing could be more white), but appear to have done so beforehand, as if a bona fide gift of the gods or, better, a divinity in itself. Pure white surfaces are *made* – like the myth of modernism's unbiased universality – constructed through years of exclusion and erasure in order to appear natural, prior and original. These contradictions manifest most explicitly in the work of architectural modernists like Adolf Loos and, in the case of whiteness, Le Corbusier.

Le Corbusier's colours

Echoing Loos' theory of 'Ornament and Crime', Swiss-born architect Le Corbusier (born Charles-Édouard Jeanneret, 1887–1965) wrote in 1925 that a 'plain coat of white Ripolin' – a commercial brand of antibacterial paint – is an 'important act in life', a force of 'productive morality'[9] that removes darkness and 'all that is not correct'.[10] It is not difficult to find such incendiary and racially charged statements throughout his writings; the challenge now is illustrating how and when Le Corbusier's celebration of *colour* fed into and contradicted broader paradigms of white power.[11]

Ripolin was a start. In architectural modernism, the deadening whiteness of synthetic chemistry came to achieve a paradigmatic status after the 1920s, namely through Le Corbusier's calls for compulsory cleaning, again waxed by overtly racist declarations that 'colour… is suited to simple races, peasants and savages'.[12]

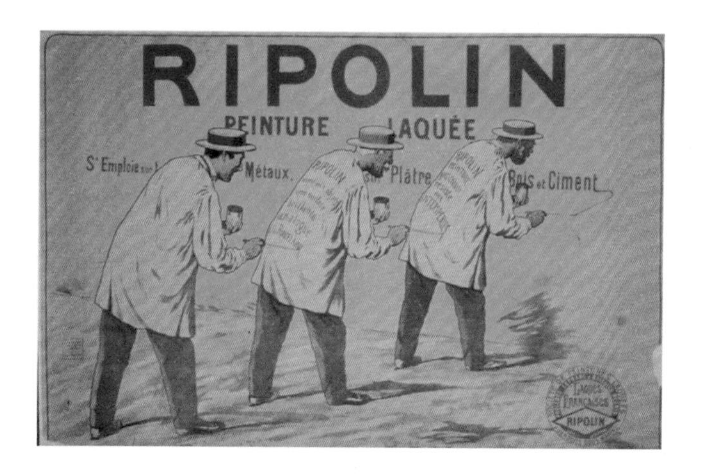

'Let's be done with it,' he continued in 1925. 'Every citizen' should be required to 'replace his hangings, his damasks, his wall-papers, his stencils, with a plain coat of white Ripolin', so that French (or German) society can spot and purge all coloured Others not like it.[13] This synthetic 'purity' became the moral code for modern whiteness.

But let us not forget that such 'superior' whitening practices were first developed in the East, only attributed to Le Corbusier and modernism after the fact. As a young student, Le Corbusier (still known then as Ch-E Jeanneret) enthusiastically studied pattern and colour,[14] only able to observe 'pure' whitewashing once he left the West in 1911 to travel East. Between May and November, Le Corbusier and Auguste Klipstein visited Asia Minor, the Balkans, Constantinople (Istanbul), southern Italy and Greece. Their 'Voyage d'Orient' began with the goal to reject Western mythologies of the East as 'unclean' and 'filthy'.[15] Le Corbusier anticipated visiting the 'great white walls of temples' in Constantinople, Asia Minor, Greece and southern Italy, all sites that – he believed – would help him dismiss the 'gossamer architecture' he disliked in the north.[16]

This goal was forgotten, however, once colour entered the scene. Le Corbusier's travel journals offer far-reaching, poetic reports on the Mediterranean's rich and sensuous golds, its moist air and earth, akin to an 'ideally shaped vase from which the heart's most profound feelings will flow'. Such colours 'elude reason', he wrote, serving only as 'a source of light, joy and... living strength'.[17] These magical hues invoked for him a celebration of life at its most vital, as they did for Hippocrates and Aristotle before him. Until they didn't.

Above: Close-up of columns in the Parthenon, Acropolis, Athens.

Opposite Left: Eugène Charles Paul Vavasseur, Ripolin painters' poster for Ripolin lacquered paint, 1898.

Right: Parthenon, Acropolis, Athens, 5th century BC, seen from the northwest, circa 1960. Photograph by Bernard Hugh Cox. The remnants falsely led historians and archaeologists to believe for centuries that the ancient pagan temple was exclusively white.

Le Corbusier, *Study of the Acropolis,* in watercolour and pencil, 1911. Instead of seeing pure white polish to plaster in the Acropolis, Le Corbusier rendered the beautiful colours of the sky and trees as they reflected off of these solid surfaces, creating an overall intoxication of colour in the icon and presumed cradle of Western civilisation.

Deadly beauty

The colours of the lifeworld soon proved too overbearing for Le Corbusier, catapulting him over the threshold of reason into what can only be described as a pseudo-psychedelic trip, enhanced by the resin wine he drank along the way.[18]

On the last leg of the journey in Greece, the belief in fixed structure and form seemed to have entirely dissolved. In Athens, Le Corbusier noted the striking colours he saw reflected off the Parthenon's surface, rendering it in his journal in pinks, reds, yellows and greens. His vivid re-interpretation of the Western monument is almost unrecognisable, though ironically, its vivid colours are more historically accurate than many illustrations thereafter. Subtle clues are offered in an outline of three black steps, vertical bars signifying columns and a receding backdrop indicating height, essentially loose lines hardly indicative of a mighty empire that once sat supreme in the continent.

By the end of his journey, Le Corbusier asserted he could even see colours without looking. With 'eyes half closed', he contended, one could give way 'to the intoxication of the fantastic glazes, the burst of yellows, the velvet tone of the blues'.[19] Again like Aristotle and Goethe before him, Le Corbusier likened his surrender to colour as being caught in an 'animated fight between brutal black masses and victorious white elements'.[20] Even if this was only a colour memory, recorded once he was back in safe and sober Switzerland, it is still remarkable to see the placement of architectural colour

Le Petit Journal

ADMINISTRATION
61, RUE LAFAYETTE, 61
Les manuscrits ne sont pas rendus
On s'abonne sans frais dans tous les bureaux de poste

5 CENT. SUPPLÉMENT ILLUSTRÉ 5 CENT.

23me Année — Numéro 1.150

DIMANCHE 1er DÉCEMBRE 1912

ABONNEMENTS

	SIX MOIS	UN AN
SEINE et SEINE-ET-OISE..	2 fr.	3 fr. 50
DÉPARTEMENTS..........	2 fr.	4 fr. »
ÉTRANGER	2 50	5 fr. »

LE CHOLÉRA

Le Petit Journal, 1 December 1912, cover. The cover of this French newspaper depicts the colours of darkness and death that overtook troops as the cholera epidemic dimmed the opulent colours of the East.

Le Corbusier, *Study of Pattern and Colour in Ornamentation*, 1911. Contrary to conventional accounts of Le Corbusier's exclusively white aesthetic, in his 1911 'Journey to the East', he explored and celebrated vivid colour.

at the *centre* of Le Corbusier's experience, between the extremes of white and black, where colour remains alive and vital. It was as if colour undid the sanctity of modern whiteness from within the site of its own expulsion.

Colour had pushed Le Corbusier too far. A sobering coat of whitewash was inevitable, if not *en route*, then certainly by the time the grey ethos of Western Europe befell him again. Arguably, the belief in transcendental white supremacy was percolating in Le Corbusier's psyche the whole time, temporarily nullified by its insatiable need to cull novel forms of entertainment from the whimsical ways of (Eastern) Others and claim them for its own (arguably, a legacy put into play since Owen Jones' 1856 *Grammar of Ornament*). While in the East, Le Corbusier seemed to shed an otherwise enduring position of white (European, colonial) selfhood to allow himself to be (temporarily) seduced by its polychromatic spectacles. Once they got too close, however, he grew sick, put his white coat back on and cast them aside again.

Near the end of the journey in Constantinople, Le Corbusier records himself fully immersed in the deadening colours of disease as the effects of the 1911 cholera epidemic were 'sweeping all the East', rendering him unable to 'hold' colour's beauty anymore. He reports having seen 'dead bodies being carried away' on the streets, 'faces exposed, green and covered with flies'.[21] More frequent references to dirt and bedbugs appear and then a full-blown transition into encounters with intolerable dirty walls, squalid interiors, noxious smells and 'diarrhoea, delirium and disorientation'.[22]

Le Corbusier and Klipstein were next forced into quarantine in Constantinople before absconding for safety in Athens. Shortly thereafter, however, they were forced into a second 'stinking quarantine' for four days on the island of St George. The colours of the East had grown darker by the day and blue skies turned 'black'.[23]

How could the notion of a safe and pure, sanitised white utopia *not* re-lodge itself as an imaginary reprieve, an idealised haven to return home to after a risqué dalliance with the Orientalism of the Other? Within four years of his return, Le Corbusier confirmed as much, declaring, 'All that bric-a-brac [from the East] I treasured disgusts me now.'[24] Once again, whiteness won.

Sanitary polychrome

Imported into Western Europe, the sanitising power of whiteness reappeared as somehow 'free' (under erasure) to refashion itself as essentially universal, modern and, in the spirit of chromophobia proper, retroactively projected onto the history and theory of colour.[25] By 1923, Le Corbusier had taken on the name by which we know him today and had begun collaborating with French painter Amédée Ozenfant (1917–1925) to co-author a truly whitewashed theory of colour under the auspices of 'Purism'. The bulk of their work together consisted of writings, paintings and architectural projects made between 1918 and 1925 and most notably their book, *Après le Cubisme* (1918), articulating the Purist ideals in conjunction with the first Purist exhibition held at the Galerie Thomas in Paris in 1918. A series of articles in the magazine *L'Esprit Nouveau*, founded by Belgian writer Paul Dermée (1886–1951) furthered the Purist mission, including offerings from such well-known figures as Fernand Léger and Paul Signac.

While feigning itself as an architectural theory of colour, Purism actively convicted colour, and décor, as 'poisons' that destroyed the natural integrity of an edifice or canvas alike. Their officially sanctioned colours, known as the 'large gamma' or 'major scale', consisted of muted hues like yellow ochre, sienna natural, sienna burned, ultramarine blue, white, black and a selection of equally low-chroma derivatives, defined in contrast to a number of modern aesthetic movements that celebrated the synthetic nature of chemical colourings.[26] Purism's secondary hues, used with much less frequency, were brighter, in what they called the 'dynamic scale', containing a 'disturbing' citron yellow, orange, vermilion and other 'animated' and 'agitated' colours while their tertiary palette (the 'transitional scale') included tinted hues like madder, emerald green and the colours of the lakes.[27]

The Purist mandate for austere, objective portrayals of everyday mass-produced objects turned on a provocative rejection of almost all related art styles and movements of the time. Their rejection of Cubism, for instance, was based on its capacity to render multiple points of view on a single two-dimensional plane, while their dismissal of Neo-Impressionism turned on what they presumed to be an inaccurate rendering of perceptual light and colour (ironically akin to Le Corbusier's intoxicated renderings of the Parthenon).[28] Cubism also lacked an essential 'narrative aspect', they argued, exhibiting 'no difference whatsoever between the aesthetics of a carpet and that of a Cubist painting'.[29] Even Fernand Léger, whom the Purists worked closely with on early issues of *L'Esprit Nouveau*, took an approach to architectural colour they dismissed as too 'ornamental' and unmodern. In essence, Purism aspired to use simple, flat, geometric forms to achieve a universal, ahistorical colour aesthetic of and for industrial machinery[30] – the epitome of the 'modern style' that Le Corbusier elsewhere internationalised.

By 1924, Le Corbusier and Ozenfant left the magazine, though their demands to strip down colourful interiors remained intact. To 'be master of yourself [and your house]... to be precise, to be accurate, [and] to think clearly',[31] Le Corbusier declared in his 1925 'Law of Ripolin', whitewash was a prerequisite. In short, Purism was not a widespread success. Its failures were not merely due to its bare-boned approach to design, or the wish to discard the materialisms of the past, but also, the fact that the Purists leveraged their pursuits *through colour* – the most ephemeral and structure-defying visual phenomenon that humans have access to. There is also the irony that the Purists' attempt to celebrate the new by dismissing the past turned on a retroactive recuperation of classical geometric ideals (yet another coat of whitewash lost in the mix).

Such contradictions inundate Le Corbusier's most famed period from the 1920s through the 1930s, when he preached the necessity of whitewash, while implementing Purism's preapproved colours to the extreme. The Pavillon de l'Esprit Nouveau (1925), for instance, was painted in nine different colours (white, black, light grey, dark grey, yellow ochre, pale yellow ochre, burnt sienna, dark burnt sienna and light blue)[32] while his Pavillon des Temps Nouveau (1937) displayed mini polychromatic spectacles with a red-painted canvas backdrop, a green wall on the left, a grey one on the right side, an entrance painted in blue, a roof made of translucent yellow materials and a floor of yellow gravel. Le Corbusier justified such decisions by claiming that a 'little' bit of colour retroactively solidified the centrality of white. Or, as he put it in 1926, 'My house will only appear white when I have placed the driving forces of colours and values in the right places... The white, which makes you think clearly, is supported by the powerful tonicity of the colour.'[33] He was not incorrect. It is only by naming colours 'Other' that axiomatic whiteness could retain its false supposition of axiomatic superiority. His chosen, 'Purist' tones drew only from 'Nature', remaining measured, safe and controllable within their confines. It is also likely that he drew from his psychedelic experiences in the East a few years prior, when *too* much colour overwhelmed him to the point of delirium. Only

a dash would now suffice as a gentle reminder of what must be tamed and controlled in the ordered world of the 'authentically' whitewashed West.

The overbearing whiteness of modern architecture was not all Le Corbusier's fault, after all, even though it is almost exclusively the white plaster of his Maison Citrohan model (1920), the Ozenfant Atelier (1922), the Villa La Roche (1923–25) and the Petit Maison for his parents on Lake Geneva (1924) that have been discussed and reproduced time and again, through black-and-white photography and textbooks celebrating them as modern demigods, mankind's final shedding of the belligerent colours that demand sanitation in order to think and act 'clearly'.[34] Rather, his work and theory of whiteness is only derivative of those who came before him (Loos, Jones, etc.) In modernity, whiteness in architecture rose to the status of religion, but only by whitewashing away the many Other colours, cultures and techniques that gave it shape and form. Now that this ground is (partially) cleared, future architectural criticism must continue to seriously explore the ways in which racism underpins less obvious forms of whiteness in the polychromatism of the present.[35]

Le Corbusier in his Pavillon des Temps Nouveau at the Exposition Internationale des Arts et des Techniques dans la Vie Moderne, Paris 1937. Decorated with colours from the Purist palette, this black-and-white photograph fails to reveal them.

1 Kant I, *Critique of Judgment*, trans. Pluhar WS, Indianapolis: Hackett, 1987, p 7.
2 Wigley M, 'Chronic whiteness', *Sick Architecture*, e-flux Architecture, 10 November 2020, https://www.e-flux.com/architecture/sick-architecture/360099/chronic-whiteness (accessed 23 August 2021).
3 Ibáñez JJ *et al.*, 'The Emergence', *Quaternary International*, 470, 2018, p 226–252; Wigley, 'Chronic'.
4 Wigley writes: 'Architecture incubated infectious disease by hosting new infra- and inter-species intimacies. Domestic cohabitation between humans and non-humans acted as a medium for inventing and exchanging disease, as well as a reservoir for storing it.' 'Chronic' n/p.
5 Wigley, 'Chronic' n/p. (Kane's italics).
6 'Ur' is a prefix typically referring to an original form or archetype.
7 Hippocrates, 'Airs, waters, places', in *Ancient Medicine. Airs, Waters, Places. Epidemics 1 and 3. The Oath. Precepts. Nutriment,* trans. Jones WHS, Loeb Classical Library 147, Cambridge, MA: Harvard University Press, 1923, part 19–20.
8 Aristotle, 'On colours', in *Minor Works*, trans. Hett WS, Loeb Classical Library 307, Cambridge, MA: Harvard University Press, 1936, p 23.
9 Le Corbusier, *L'Art decoratif d'aujourd'hui*, Paris: Editions Crès, 1925; trans. Dunnett J as *The Decorative Art of Today*, Cambridge: MIT Press, 1987, p 189.
10 Le Corbusier, *L'Art decoratif*, p 188.
11 In his late life, Le Corbusier returned to colour, at first through his two sets of Sallubra wallpapers (1931 and 1959), and in 1958, with his work on the Pavillon Philips at the Brussels World Fair.
12 Le Corbusier, *Towards a New Architecture*, London: Architectural Press, 1927, p 143.
13 See Hammer I, 'White, everything white? Josef Frank's Villa Beer (1930) in Vienna, and its materiality in the context of the discourse on "white cubes"', *Built Heritage* 4(2), 2020, p 1–16.
14 Flores notes how Le Corbusier paid 'particular attention to the use of colour to assist the definition of form' and sensation in Owen Jones' work. Flores CAH, *Owen Jones: Design, Ornament, Architecture*, New York: Rizzoli, 2006, p 252.
15 Jeanneret C-E, 'Quelques impressions', *La Feuille d'Avis de La Chaux-de-Fonds*, 20 July 1911.
16 Jeanneret, 'Quelques impressions'; Wigley, 'Chronic' n/p.
17 Le Corbusier, *Le Voyage d'Orient*, 1966; trans. Žaknić I as *Journey to the East*, Cambridge: MIT Press, 1987, pp 14, 234; Wigley, 'Chronic' n/p.
18 'I must have drank too much resin wine… Again today I imbibed too much resin wine.' Resin wine was a precursor to absinthe, prohibited in France since 1930. Le Corbusier, *Journey to the East*, p 235.
19 Le Corbusier, 'A Letter to friends', in *Journey to the East*, p 14.
20 Ibid.
21 Le Corbusier, *Journey to the East*, p 235.
22 'On the bedsheets' at his Turkish hotel, he writes, 'the black of the bedbugs [were] easily equal to the weight of the unwashed linen,' Le Corbusier, *Journey to the East*, p 82; pp 88, 93, 142.
23 Le Corbusier, *Journey to the East*, p 235.
24 Weber NF, 'Charles-Édouard Jeanneret to William Ritter', 1 November 1911, in *Le Corbusier: A Life*, New York: Alfred A Knopf, 2008, p 99.
25 'In the course of my travels… I found whitewash wherever the twentieth century had not yet arrived,' [that is, *pure* whitewash, *original* whitewash, as anything *but* modern], Le Corbusier, *The Decorative Art,* p 189.
26 Le Corbusier and Ozenfant A, 'Purism', 1964, in Herbert RL (ed), *Modern Artists on Art*, New York: Dover, 2000, pp 62–64.
27 Scavuzzo G, 'Compositions for chromatic keyboards: Colour and composition in Le Corbusier's works', in *Proceedings of the Colour and Light in Architecture Conference,* Venice, 2010, p 434.
28 Braham WW, *Modern Colour/Modern Architecture*, London: Routledge, 2002, p 2.
29 Jeanneret C-E and Ozenfant A, *Après le Cubisme*, Paris: Altamira, 1918, repr. 1999, p 27.
30 That these same industrial machines also produced the same gamut of industrial colours that they rejected was somehow lost to them.
31 Le Corbusier, *The Decorative Art,* p 188.
32 Batchelor D, *Chromophobia*, London: Reaktion Books, 2000, p 47.
33 Le Corbusier, 'Notes a la suite', Cahiers d'art 3, p 49; also cited in Wigley, 'Chronic' n/p.
34 Le Corbusier, *The Decorative Art,* p 188.
35 An expansive exploration of these concepts appears in Kane CL, *Electrographic Architecture: New York Color, Las Vegas Light, and America's White Imaginary*, Berkeley CA: University of California Press, 2023.

Collective Palettes: On Colour and Identity

Courtney Coffman

We could learn, then, to feast our monochromatic eyes on colour, and in the process come to love a difference.[1]

Historically, the paradox of colour is whether it is objective or subjective. Cultural codifications and identities are inherent in colour, and this may explain the recent surge in books on colour histories and theories, like Kassia St Clair's *The Secret Lives of Colour* (2017), N. Khandekar *et al's An Atlas of Rare and Familiar Colour: The Harvard Art Museums' Forbes Pigment Collection Paperback* (2019) or David Cole's *Chromatopia: An Illustrated History of Colour* (2021),[2] among many others. Often represented in diagrammatic geometries of wheels, pyramids, hexagons, stars and squares, early colour theories came from other disciplinary fields beyond architecture.[3] Yet within these micro-histories of colour, broader topics have emerged that are just as pertinent to the design field today: colonialism, taxonomy, intellectual property, classism and gender. Given the multiplicity of individual 'selves' that exist today – our analogue self, our digital self and the gradient in-between – the current interest in colour as a signifier helps us project our identity and communicate our self-prescribed ideologies. Architecture, too, can simultaneously capture both the objective and the subjective, eliciting yet another binary: distinguishing differences or celebrating shared sensibilities.

Jerald Cooper subverting the historical canon: Solange atop a pink-rendered Guggenheim.

But first, pink!

For nearly 10 years we've been gleefully drowning in the soft hue of a particular fleshy variety, commonly known as 'Millennial Pink'. It began trickling into the online feeds of Tumblr blogs and early Instagram posts, reworking the tween-forward baby pink of Y2K and muddling it with a tinge of grey. The resulting neutralised shade became ubiquitous with a new aesthetic language, one with strong postmodern underpinnings whose flatness and postmodern, Memphis-like shapes proved successful for virtual consumption. 'Museums' – of ice cream, colour factories, 29 rooms – and other immersive, pop-up experiences or physical spaces capitalised on this colour as mere backdrop 'for the gram'. Millennial Pink became associated with bodacious decorative objects and *vibes*, emerging alongside a new wave of exploration in self-identity that actually seemed to hold our cultural and consumer attention for an extended period of time.

The continued success of Millennial Pink also coincides with the moment in which everyday people began to co-opt a certain rhetoric and extroversion on social media platforms – exchanging thoughts of random

Praised as 'a true hero' on Instagram, graffiti artist Thrash sends a clear message to the influencer ilk on The Pink Wall of the Paul Smith store in LA: 'Go Fuck Ur Selfie'.

sincerity for highly curated content: subjectivity as brand identity. Alongside this emerging visual culture, consumer markets cashed in on the speed of digital media trends, hiring 'brand ambassadors' and other up-and-coming social media influencers who often emulated celebrities (i.e. affordable endorsements for expansive product placement). And one way to flatten the distinction among these unknown individuals was through the semiotics and Millennial Pink was an instantly identifiable commodity. Dominating clothing, accessories, housewares, furniture, publications, food, beverages and so on, Millennial Pink launched numerous entrepreneurial endeavours – like 'clean' skincare and make-up – and refreshed established brands as they donned this rosy tint, like Apple's rollout of its Rose Gold products.

From the Baroque to the Bauhaus, every zeitgeist carries a new a colour scheme based on material resources, economies and culture, and despite the vapidity of posts and instantaneous stories, there is just as much a codification in the use of colour in contemporary times, particularly as we navigate our digital and analogue worlds in tandem. It would seem that media outlets and writers also picked up on the global dominance and cultural enthusiasm of Millennial Pink and its passive yet underlyingly aggressive tone. Bloggers, media theorists, even *The New York Times* covered the monochromatic popularity of pink and its history.[4] Alongside the heavy rotation of ubiquitous pink spaces proliferating online, influencers found more obscure places for their feeds and photoshoots. Thanks to Instagram and the power of pink, 'undiscovered' projects started to appear in personal posts and advertising campaigns, like Luis Barragán's 1968 Cuadra San Cristóbal, an equestrian estate northeast of Mexico City, and La Muralla Roja, a 1973 multifamily housing project in Alicante by Spanish architect Ricardo Bofill. And unfamiliar histories (to younger generations) resurfaced, like how Rem Koolhaas worked alongside Arquitectonica's Laurinda Spear on the iconic Pink House in Miami, that Frank Gehry's home in Santa Monica was originally clad in a mauvy-salmon that peeks out from under its sculptural facade, or the discovery that Frank Lloyd Wright rendered a proposal for the Guggenheim to be pink. My favourite post of the latter being an a-historical swerve by Jerald Cooper, who runs the Instagram handle @hoodmidcenturymodern, who photoshopped a giantess Solange atop a rose-tinted Guggenheim, claiming her space as a Black woman over the familiar whitewashed building.

Eventually, Millennial Pink's trendiness-turned-everydayness became predictable as it recycled through the same channels, and its use as an active tool of politicised communication became diluted by its repetition and frequent absorption. It seems the world has moved on: the '#girlboss' is no longer the (only) influencer and the pink of our pop-cultural imagination apparently has become too basic for us to collectively enjoy. The result of this transition is now trickling into our physical spaces as well – the most Insta-famous example being the Gallery room in Sketch London, which made headlines in 2022 as it swapped its 2014 Millennial Pink interior for a sunny yellow, no doubt attracting teatime tourism to this monochromatic mecca. While not an exact colour match to Millennial Pink, the generically specific pink wall at Paul Smith's Melrose boutique in Los Angeles captures the warmth of Southern California's light, taking cues from the iconic colourful walls of Mexican architect Luis Barragán. The store's prevalence among influencers in LA set off a chain reaction of wannabes and flocking tourists, especially once Instagram introduced the geotag 'The Pink Wall'. The frenzy over this one, highly accessible public wall on commercial property required Paul Smith to bulk up on car park security and traffic control as selfie-seekers had a major impact during peak photography hours where golden hour and gridlock happened to coincide. Paul Smith has attempted to seasonally revamp the 2005 bold pink facade with subtle interventions, likely to gesture that The Pink Wall is attached to an actual store, but this hasn't thwarted the crowds as much as the brazen work of one graffiti artist.

An amplified pink

Along with the surge in Millennial Pink came a major shift in identity politics: its subtle hue was fully charged, seemingly retaliating against the dominate patriarchal paradigm. Since the post-war period, pink has been flatly categorised as simply 'girly' or 'feminine'; it was also used to label and subsequently oppress the gay community, and has now come to represent LGBTQ+ visibility and liberation. The androgyny of Millennial Pink challenged this status quo and its codifications. The late designer Virgil Abloh testified to the cultural power and perception of pink in an interview with writer Earlwyn Covington:

I'm colour sensitive. Colour is at the root of art and design. Colour immediately gives you an emotion and it's no coincidence that one of my major projects is called Off-White. When it comes to the colour pink, it reaches back to what you possessed in childhood when your brain becomes programmed that pink is feminine and blue masculine. I think in that short narrative, there lies the root of my artistic practice, which is to sort out these preconceived notions based on opted truths, which as you get older you realise are not found on anything factual, just consensus.[5]

Coming out of the pandemic, vibrant variations of fuchsia and the hottest of pinks have come full-force in recent fashion collections. For his dual-gender Autumn/Winter 2022 collection, Valentino's creative director Pierpaolo Piccioli showcased 40 designs in a singular hot pink (with touches of black) among a matching architectural set covered carpet to column. Piccioli reveals, 'I always want pink in my collections. It's a colour I feel you can subvert better, because it already has a lot of meaning. It changed during the centuries: it was the colour of the power of men, then it became girlish… I like to subvert the idea. Today, it means different things.'[6]

Further, savvy Piccioli paired up with Pantone – the colour-forecasting folks – who collaborated on this particular hue and catalogued it in their colour library as Pink PP. This commercial aspect suggests that Piccioli is not just interested in using pink seasonally, but is attempting to contextualise it indefinitely through institutional means. Only time will tell whether this move to secure Pink PP's place in Pantone's catalogue is one of chromatic posterity or pure hubris.

Fashion editors translated the emergence of this bright pink as more than mere peacocking after isolation, but rather as a determined consumer choice of feminine protestation against the many laws and

Mamani's colourful 'New Andean' architectural style has proliferated across the monochromatic El Alto, demonstrating the economic growth and prosperity of the city's Indigenous population.

regulations recently inflicted on bodies and rights. By clothing both the models and the architecture in a shocking pink, Piccioli purposefully redirected attention to the individuals wearing the garments – establishing singularity among uniformity.

Chromocity

I first learned about the architecture of Freddy Mamani Silvestre in El Alto, Bolivia thanks to Andrew Kovacs, who runs the notorious Tumblr and Instagram accounts *Archive of Affinities*, and subsequentially taught a Travelling Studio for Master of Architecture students at the University of California, Los Angeles in the autumn of 2018, titled 'Learning from Freddy Mamani...(insider/ outsider architecture)'. For years, Kovacs has mined old publications and archival materials for the 'deep cuts' and 'B-sides' of architecture's past, and understood that beyond the spectacle of Mamani's buildings, their presence among the monochromatic brick urban fabric of El Alto offered a certain sincerity through an architectural form and colour.

My first impression of Mamani's buildings is that they reminded me of the Transformer-like Dekotora (or 'decoration trucks') in Japan, with all their shiny chrome, colourful LED lights and edging details, layers upon layers of geometries that no doubt represent a highly specific subculture of individuals. Mamani's architecture is equally highly specific in its ornamental articulation, programming and execution; he specialises in one particular building typology, called the 'Cholet'. Embracing the common insult of 'cholo', a derogatory word for a rural migrant, and crossing it with 'chalet', harking back to the pitched roofs and ornamental facades found in his projects, Mamani has created a new architectural style for a growing middle class. Deemed 'New Andean', Mamani's mark on the city can been seen in more than 80 of his Cholets, alongside multiple imitators and copies popping up across El Alto.

The highest and second-largest city in Bolivia, El Alto is a warm, earth-toned city backdropped by mountains, mostly comprised of common mud-brick and metal-roof construction – a cost-efficient means for the government to accommodate the influx of residents and development in the last decade. Within the city's homogenous urban fabric, which sits just west of the more affluent La Paz, the one million residents of El Alto are primarily Indigenous peoples of Aymara and Quechua origin; known as 'Alteños', they are urban citizens yet maintain their land rights outside the city, and they celebrate their culture through parades,

Bolivia's 'traditional' flag and the Wiphala (pan-Indigenous) flag of Bolivia.

Mamani's chromatic variations in each project are specific to each site, based on the client's personal taste and vision.

music, costumes and, most importantly, colour. It's interesting to consider that in tandem with El Alto's growth, Bolivia's first elected Indigenous president, Evo Morales, ushered in a new national flag: the pan-Indigenous Wiphala – a numeric array of squares in seven distinctive colours, each representative of Andean culture and collective identity.[7] The sentiment of shared values among Indigenous communities has proved beneficial as El Alto has experienced major economic development over the last decade.[8] Expression of this newfound wealth and independence comes in the form of architecture: the Cholet captures both the unique culture and recent upward mobility of the Aymara bourgeoise.

Mamani's Cholets are mixed-use and while they vary from five to six storeys in height, they follow similar programmatic functions. Designed to sustain income generation for the owners, the ground level is the most public and offers daily commercial spaces, such as bodegas and storage spaces for the party equipment that is then used in the Salon de Eventos – double-height Party Halls that host numerous celebrations, an important component for Aymaran public life.[9] Topping out the Cholet is the residential component: this may consist of apartments on the top floor – where extended family and members of the community may rent from the owners – but it also includes the smaller house (the 'chalet') whose geometries are independent from those on the primary facade, which take their cues from the Andean forms of ancient Pre-Colombian sites, like Tiwanaku. The facades' multicoloured patterns and glass finishes forge a distinctive connection between Andean art and the present-day El Alto. Mamani reveals, 'My architecture seeks to find my city an identity by rescuing and using certain formal elements of our Indigenous culture.'[10]

Mamani's vivacious exteriors are a modest foreshadowing of the exuberant, technicolour spaces within. Form and light make the colours vibrate, as softly curved shapes meet the crisp edges of a cornice; their meeting is highlighted by the pop of contrasting lines that emphasise their dramatic geometries. Some of the colours remain solid in application, while others are expressed with the wispy gradient of an airbrush, flourished with hand-painted flowers and lines that render the ceilings as confectionary eye candy. In observing the construction progress photos of these projects, with their undulating ceilings and hypostyle-like columns rendered in a dull, chalky finish, it's apparent how impactful the bold and bright colour

While often imitated, Mamani identifies and boasts the three-dimensionality of his buildings, expressed in the articulation of the facade and the massing of the owner's 'chalet' on top.

palette is to the atmosphere and life of the Cholets. Reinforcing the inexorable link between colour and identity, the dominant colour of each Cholet is often selected by the owner, which explains the diverse rainbow sprinkled across the city.

Transformational colour

The cross-pollination of traditional costume and Mamani's work can be seen in his 2018 installation at the Fondation Cartier in Paris. When he was invited to re-create a Cholet within the gallery, Mamani pondered, 'What is a Cholet without its *Cholita*?' (Cholitas are Indigenous Bolivian women.) This prompted a collaboration with Indigenous couture designer Ana Palza, who created a collection inspired by the architecture of Mamani's Cholets. The resulting fashion show was a meta-architectural moment: Cholitas swished down the runway, showcasing Palza's interpretation of Mamani's architecture on the modelled garments, colourful facades printed as borders on the plaited *pollera* skirts and on shawls wrapping their shoulders, all within a faux-Cholet in the Fondation's gallery. Some of the shawls were printed with photo-elevations of the Cholets, while others were of the Cholitas themselves posing inside a Party Hall in full costume; my favourite were the hand-stitched ornamental patterns that abstracted specific facade details.

In his 2019 presentation at The Met's annual symposium, 'In Our Time: A Year of Architecture in a Day', Mamani described the layers of colour and pattern of the Cholets as being inspired by the traditional *pollera*, the skirts worn by Indigenous Bolivian women, or Cholitas. I was whisked away with the whimsical thought of some 80-plus buildings projecting the feminine image of these colourful handmade skirts, softening the hardness of a monolith brick-and-mortar city; I also imagined the owner's house atop the Cholet as a hat – a wink at the *bombín* (bowler hat) also worn by the Cholitas.

At the conclusion of his presentation, Mamani screened the trailer for Isaac Niemand's documentary, *Cholet: The Work of Freddy Mamani*. Filmed in 2016, it was clear that Mamani was already a sensation and had cemented Indigenous cultural identity in El Alto's built environment at the time of Niemand's project. In the full-length documentary, Niemand captures a variety of responses from numerous people, including Mamani and his critics. It's clear that those who dismiss Mamani's designs as simply 'kitsch' are no doubt basing their observations on the exact entrenched pedagogies

Punctuated with light and expanded by reflection, Mamani's technicolour architecture is amplified through cultural motifs and forms, such as the Indigenous Wiphala flag echoing on the columns.

MUJERES
VARONES
DAMAS

A Cholita stands inside one of Mamani's Salons de Eventos, privately owned spaces that host Indigenous community celebrations.

of Western architectures that Mamani is attempting to distance himself from. While some of his critics acknowledge (or at least cannot deny) Mamani's success, given the numerous projects throughout El Alto, they distinguish the notion of 'kitsch' primarily because of the colours used in the projects. Yet as I sat in The Met's packed auditorium, the audience was engrossed in this immersive, polychromic architecture. A short scene of Mamani dancing inside one of the Cholets made the audience burst into a resounding awe, and just then, Mamani began dancing on stage. The entire auditorium stood up, clapping with joy – a standing ovation for an architecture of acknowledgement.

Mamani's buildings and their colourful facades showcase the pride of their Indigenous owners. It is fascinating, then, to witness the reaction to this architecture – much like pink, it elicits either pure joy or contempt – few occupy the 'neutral' category. Unlike Millennial Pink, many of us won't be able to experience Mamani's colours first-hand to determine whether his architecture should be understood as objective or subjective, but if I had to guess, it happily lands in the middle, a colourful centrism.

1 Andreoli E and D'Andrea L, *La Arquitectura de Freddy Mamani Silvestre*, La Paz: Artes Gráficas Sagitario SRL, 2014, p 33.
2 St Clair K, *The Secret Lives of Colour*, New York: Penguin Books, 2017; Khandekar N *et al.*, *An Atlas of Rare and Familiar Colour: The Harvard Art Museums' Forbes Pigment Collection Paperback*, Los Angeles: Atelier Éditions, 2019; Cole D, *Chromatopia: An Illustrated History of Colour*, New York: Thames & Hudson, 2019 and 2021.
3 Most early colour theory is attributed to the fields of science and philosophy, and figurers such as Isaac Newton and Johann Wolfgang von Goethe, who were the seminal colour theorists until the early 20th century, when the Bauhaus and its students (including Josef Albers) conducted courses exclusively in colour theory.
4 David Byrne contributed an essay on pink for the editorial column 'Colours', in *Cabinet Magazine*; see Byrne D, 'Colours/Pink: Not so sweet afterall', *Cabinet Magazine* 11, 2003, https://www.cabinetmagazine.org/issues/11/byrne.php (accessed 2 November 2022).
5 Covington E, 'Pinking Virgil: The B-side', *Damn Magazine* 76, 2020, p 131.
6 Madsen AC, '5 things to know about Valentino's hot pink AW22 show', *Vogue*, 7 March 2022, https://www.vogue.co.uk/fashion/gallery/valentino-aw22-5-things-to-know (accessed 3 February 2023).
7 For a very through, in-depth explanation and examination of the multiplicity of meanings and colours embedded in the Wiphala, see: https://www.katari.org/pdf/wiphala.pdf (accessed 2 November 2022).
8 El Alto is considered a commercial hub; with many workshops and material merchandise exports, many of the locally owned businesses work with larger industries, some stretch as far as the global East, setting up business in Shanghai and Guangzhou, and learning Chinese to further grow.
9 In one Cholet, for example, the client requested a football (soccer) pitch, which Mamani delivered.
10 Andreoli and D'Andrea, *La Arquitectura de Freddy Mamani Silvestre*, p 25.

Digital Colour: A Semi-Technical Reflection

Galo Canizares

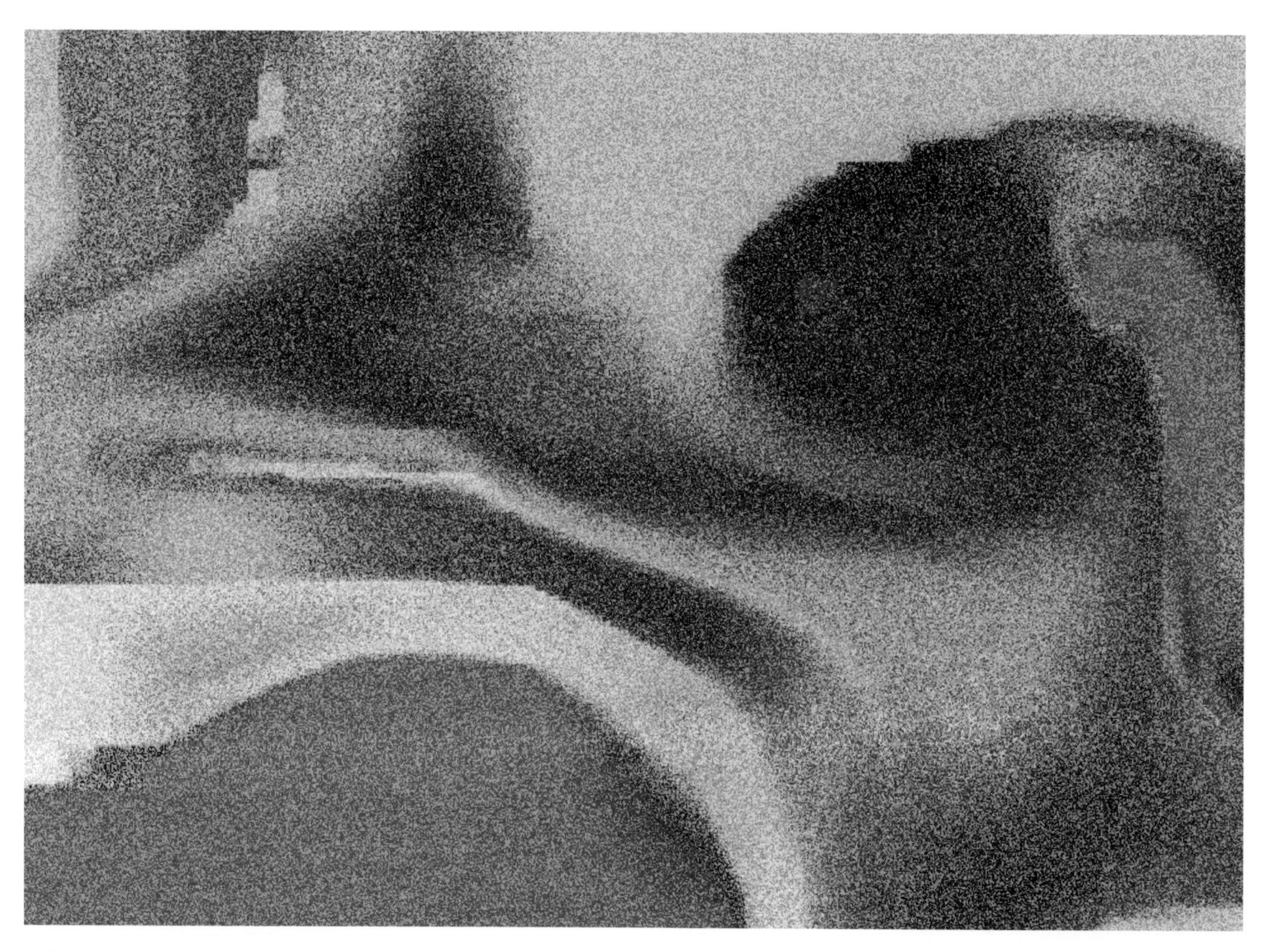

Galo Canizares, *SCREENSPACE SILICA 220404-09*, 2022. Image made with custom image-processing software.

Colour and architecture have a tenuous relationship. When colour is discussed in the context of architecture, the focus is often on cosmetics, materials or some didactic notion of visual organisation. The projects that have established themselves as canonical in their unique application of colour range from one-offs such as the Rietveld Schröder House in Utrecht (that singular foray into the potential of De Stijl painting-becoming-architecture) or stylistic flamboyance, as in the pastel hues in postmodern buildings and interiors. Moreover, projects like Casa Luis Barragán in Mexico City and the Centre Pompidou in Paris, draw visitors from all over, largely because of their respective chromatic uniqueness – the former for its painterly modernism, the latter for its techno-indexical colour-coded building system exterior. The examples could keep going, but suffice to say that discussions of colour in architecture have remained, for a large part, focused on its physical application. That is to say: despite the abundance and worldwide proliferation of screens and electronic light, little has been explored regarding the relationship of digital/electronic colour and its architectural effects or usage. This essay examines the role that colour plays in contemporary architecture through a synthesis of reflections on digital colour and architectural media from a techno-social perspective. It highlights both the phenomenological potentials as well as specific technical knowledge that must be understood in order to pursue the subject critically. This exploration emphasises a semi-technical approach that combines theoretical analysis with elementary technical background on digital colour. Understanding the feedback loop between perception and technics can help paint a cohesive picture of the role digital colour plays in contemporary architectural design.

Top: (ab)Normal, 'Chroma Park', 2022.

Middle: (ab)Normal, 'DICHO', 2020.

Left: Office CA, 'Blue, A Set Design', Boston, 2015. Custom stage set for the Boston Theater Company.

It is also crucial to note that contemporary experimental architectural practice has become somewhat synonymous with experimental visualisation. However, as architect Zeina Koreitem has noted, 'Computational images do not exist without the notion of computational colour, and vice versa. Exploring the vast territory of colourisation requires learning, and becoming literate in, the technical structure of images and computational colour, alongside (not despite) their traditional political, cultural or aesthetic realities.'[1] It is therefore unsurprising that many contemporary architectural designers have embraced advanced visualisation tools to explore innovative spatial and environmental effects. These effects, afforded largely by computer vision and image-processing software, have shifted the focus of experimentation to the production of larger-than-life or impossible scenographics.

There are two approaches that are worth exploring in discussions of digital colour: (1) the use of chroma keying techniques to layer and augment a space, and (2) the exaggeration or replication of default virtual material effects in physical spaces. The first is characterised, quite simply, by practices that build off popularised filmic chroma keying techniques for use in architectural situations. The second is characterised by practices that attempt to physicalise digital tropes by making physical spaces resembling digital visualisations, thereby creating a dialogue between physical and virtual space.

Chroma

In his 2001 *Grey Room* essay 'Computer graphics: A semi-technical introduction', media scholar Friedrich Kittler set out to answer a seemingly straightforward question: What is the difference between an image and a computer image? Kittler's answer required some technical exploration. He took a stroll through the history of computer graphics, optics and the virtualisation of optics (rendering), concluding that the mathematics underlying new modes of representation warrant just as much conceptual scrutiny as phenomenological theories of vision. 'For what philosophical aesthetics, most prominently in Kant's *Critique of Judgment*, once determined about the alleged difference between line and colour, derivation and integral', writes Kittler, 'does justice neither to paintings nor to computer graphics.'[2] In other words, 3D visualisation and rendering applications constitute a universe of positions between subjects, objects, simulated particles and projectiles that, with every technological advancement, affect how we perceive the world – just as painting and photography did. The problem, however, is that the complexity of these systems obscures as much as it reveals, making it difficult to formulate accessible theories of how they are shifting this perception.

Kittler's attempt to explain the ontology of computer graphics already predicted the kinds of sociocultural effects computer-generated imagery (CGI) and digital colour would have in the coming decades. The film industry, for example, relies so much on CGI that behind-the-scenes looks at film sets today are mostly barren blue/greenscreen scenography populated by actors adorned in registration marker suits and placeholder structures. Movie scenes come together in post-production, where the blue or green components of the scene are replaced by computer-generated environments, objects and characters. But this process, called 'chroma keying', uses colour not simply as a tool to separate actor from backdrop. It acts as a mechanism for reading the physical space of the scene and translating its colours into discrete zones of information to be replaced and/or augmented. What we see when we watch special-effects driven films is a composite image built out of many layers of information, largely organised using colour.

This is the primary conceit of the multidisciplinary design firm (ab)Normal's 2022 installation, 'Chroma Park'. As its name suggests, the project makes use of chroma keying to augment parts of the space using digital video overlays. Despite resembling a simple skateboarding half-pipe, the space can be digitally activated through screens with chroma keying software. This allows the actors and participants within the space to be projected onto another layer of images or the park to disappear altogether. (ab)Normal also deployed this spatial technique in a small installation called 'DICHO' at the Tbilisi Biennial in 2020. Taking cues from online virtual meetings where individuals use computer vision and colour filtering to separate their bodies from their backgrounds, (ab)Normal built a gathering space wrapped in a standard chroma key blue curtain. In physical space, this backdrop appeared surreal, almost sterile, but would disappear completely when used for broadcasting the gatherings within the space. More movie studio than typical architectural pavilion, the 'DICHO' and 'Chroma Park' installations highlight a culture of video filtering and scenography made possible only through the manipulation of digital colour.

The proliferation of chroma keying techniques has also standardised two colours as physical materials: key blue and key green. While they vary slightly

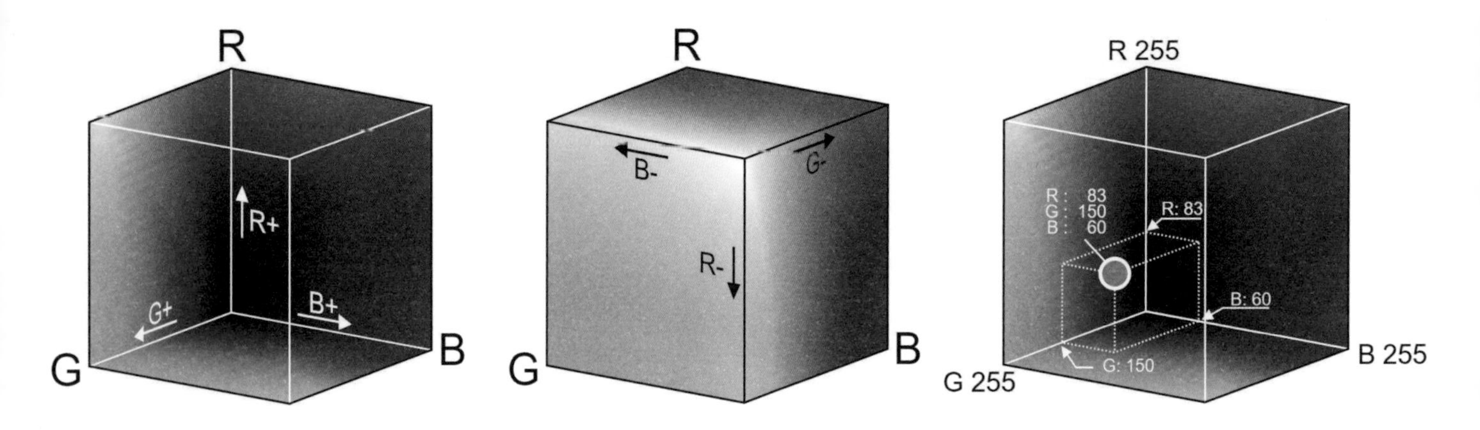

We can represent RGB in three dimensions by associating each colour with a Euclidean axis.

Below left: Paul Bourke, colour used to isolate individual geometry, 1993.

Below right: Paul Bourke, black lines generated by detecting the difference between colours in the previous image, 1993.

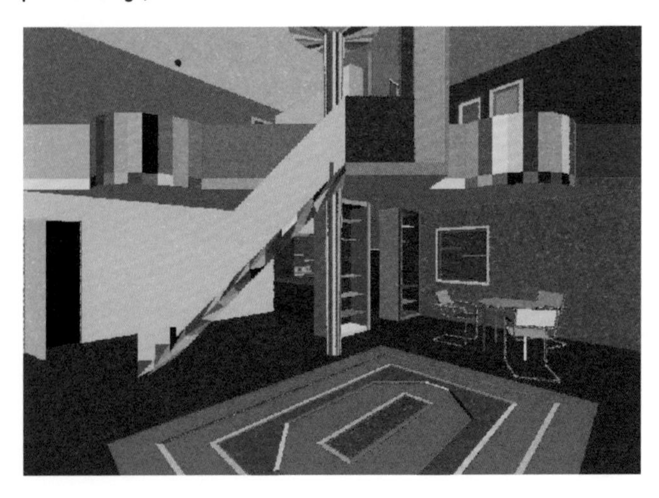

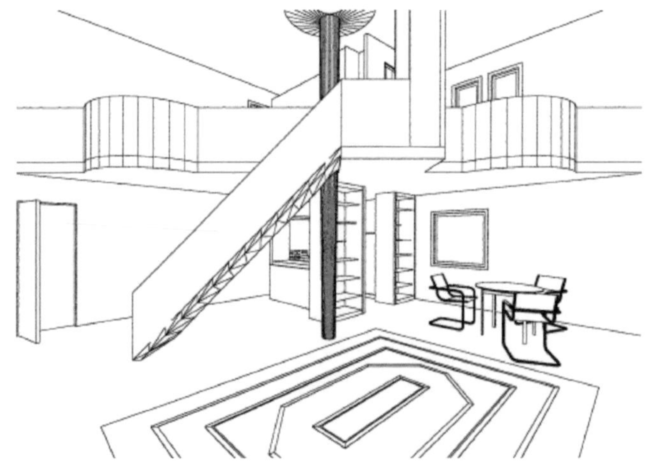

depending on their manufacture, these two bright shades of blue and green dominate the visual effects industries. So prominent are these colours in large-scale fabric manufacturing that when the architecture firm Office CA was tasked with wrapping a small theatre with fabric for the Boston Theater Company in 2015, the only colour available at such quantities was chroma key blue. The resulting stage set design thus incorporated the economics of the visual effects industry into the final design and produced a kind of meta-curtain that wrapped both performers and audience in a pure blue hue. Like in (ab)Normal's 'DICHO' installation, this fabric, typically designed to be invisible, paradoxically produced a striking, all-encompassing effect due to its hyperreal presence.

Processes of chroma keying are only possible due to the discretisation of pixel colour values into machine-legible units. But the most important aspect to note about the use of colour in visual effects is that it is premised on an optical feedback loop of image recognition and addressability. Cameras and software must be able to precisely pick out the difference between the chroma green or chroma blue and other colours at the level of the individual pixel. We can therefore state that modern computer graphics not only use colour to *represent* high-fidelity reconstructions of the world, but they also use colour to *interpret* the world itself. This is what Kittler dubbed the ontological 'that-ness and what-ness' of computer graphics or the relationships between subjects and objects – addressable coordinates, colours, viewing matrices – in virtual space. Today we call this dialogue *computer vision*: a system's ability to recognise patterns or specific information in a field of raw data. In contrast to chemical photography, the sensors in modern cameras make immediate judgements about the colour information they receive. Sensors that have been trained to perceive certain phenomena, such as depth, for example, can immediately attempt to decipher the spatial actuality of an image based solely on its colours.[3] As soon as a colour is captured, the system must decide what that colour represents, whether to compress it or not, whether to key it out or whether to adjust it.

New media artist Alan Warburton calls the outputs of these processes 'exploded images', images that contain much more than just visual information.[4] This, however, should not be confused with 'metadata', which is text embedded in the file formats of images. The 'exploded image' goes beyond text information; it is organised in layers or channels that combine this data so it may be extracted later through various post-processes. According to Warburton, colour data in exploded images performs multiple functions; it maps visual information as well as hidden data like spatial coordinates, object properties and three-dimensional manipulations. Beyond a visual phenomenon, colour has become an indexical instrument used to interpret the world around us for ourselves and for our machines.

Rendering

As Koreitem and Kittler suggest, to better understand how digital colour affects spatial experience, we must look at its technical basis. A close examination of the RGB colour model, for example, reveals how it enables us to interpret the space of an image.[5] In an additive colour model like RGB, colour mixtures are based on the accumulation of visible light: red, green and blue at their full intensity produce white. We can represent RGB in three dimensions by associating each colour with a Euclidean axis. If R (red) can be represented by X, green (G) by Y and blue (B) by Z, we can arrive at a three-dimensional model of RGB where the 0, 0, 0 coordinate is equal parts 0 of red, green and blue (aka black). Moving along those axes changes the relative mixtures of RGB. For example, moving on the X and Y axis an equal distance will eventually lead to a full mixture of R and G, which is yellow. Moving along the X and Z axis all the way will result in a full mixture of R and B, which is magenta. And so on. This spatial interpretation of the RGB colour model results in a cubic representation of colour within which any mixture of red, green and blue can be accurately measured and addressed.[6] The RGB colour cube forms the basis for a spatial understanding of digital colour.

Representing colour as a spatial coordinate has opened a new dimension of geometric and spatial reasoning in computer graphics. In architectural modelling, the RGB model allows for both indexical legibility of multiple components and the encoding of geometric information onto a surface. For early CAD programmers, the ability to use colour to distinguish between various elements in virtual space was paramount to this new way of working. At this time, colour was not used representationally, but rather purely as an organisational technique (something that remains in practice with colour-coding layers in 3D-modelling software). Because colour can be processed faster than complex geometry, it was an efficient way to produce legible visualisations. Researchers like Paul Bourke at the University of Western Australia developed methods for producing line drawings that required first visualising

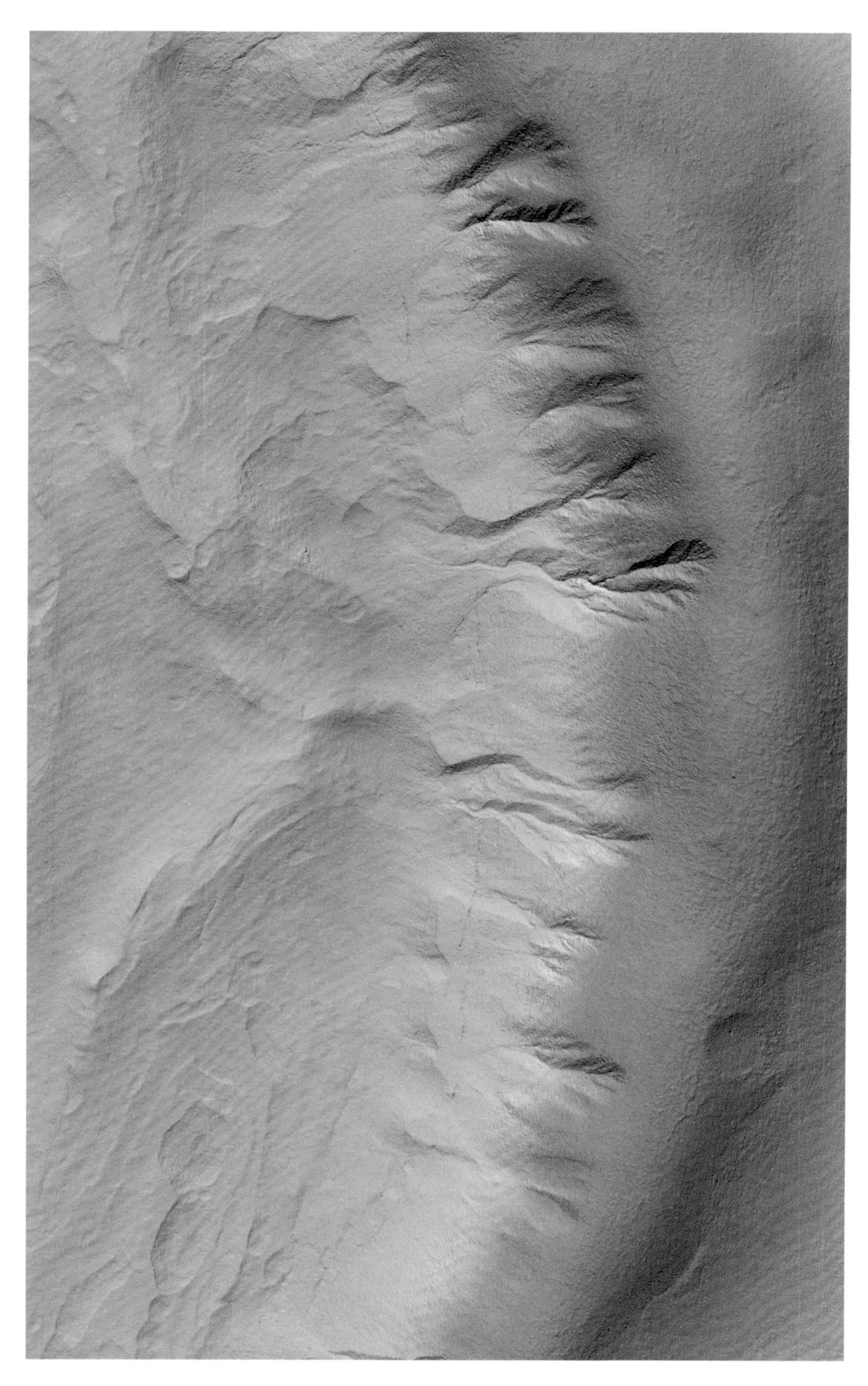

Galo Canizares, satellite image of a Martian crater, coloured according to its topographic 'normals' in space, 2017.

each component of the model as distinct RGB colours, then running an edge detection algorithm that would draw a line when a change in colour was detected, resulting in renderings that mimicked hand-drawn line perspectives without ever having to draw or draft anything.[7] A similar indexical relationship can best be seen in 'normal' – meaning a mathematical normal, a perpendicular direction – rendering techniques, where each face in a 3D geometry is coloured according to its tangential facing direction. In this mode of representation, geometry can achieve a kind of psychedelic effect as the full spectrum of RGB is used simultaneously to show changes in the surface orientation of a geometry, a rainbow-like prismatic coating meant primarily to find errors in an object's surface.

These applications of colour in digital architectural design workflows reinforce Warburton's exploded image concept. Each technique – rendering individual polygons, normal mapping – is just another layer of information made legible for a computer. For applications such as geographic information system (GIS) modelling, colours representing geometric direction are mapped onto surfaces to describe elevational changes in topography, allowing a static two-dimensional image to contain three-dimensional data, resulting in an efficient form of compression. In photorealistic visualisations, normal mapping allows the material to achieve more detail by providing simulated depth information in a compressed format. But, as normal visualisations show, they can also produce standalone effects. Normal visualisations can produce otherworldly imagery relatively easily, and while a computer may read the image in a highly logical way, human interpretation can reveal other qualities. As architects and designers begin to explore more of the exploded image, they can bring more subjective interpretations of these chromatic effects into discussions of digital imagery.

The seemingly paradoxical nature of utilising bright colours only to disappear in virtual space is further enhanced by an emerging genre of architectural projects that attempt to physicalise virtual materials. This category of work, largely influenced by the default appearance of computer renderings, has been pioneered by artists, architects and designers such as Virgil Abloh, Daniel Arsham, Roxy Paine, Xavi Aguirre and Neyran Turan (to name a few). While some may describe this genre of work simply as monochromatic, there is an incontrovertible link between the popularisation of default 'clay' rendering images from computer graphics and the dioramic content of these artists' works.

'Four Dioramas' by Neyran Turan's studio, NEMESTUDIO, look very much like computer renderings. They produce a double-take effect where an audience familiar with digital visualisations may, in fact, assume that it is an unbuilt, purely computer-rendered scene. The uncanny effects produced by painting every quotidian object in the scene, from plants to books to signage, a homogenous colour flatten the space of the scene into an assumed two-dimensional representation of itself. In these images, digital colour is referenced directly, not as a simulation of optical effects (per Kittler), but rather as a sociocultural phenomenon of visual expectations. The viewer, already subsumed in digital visualisations, expects a rendering, but is instead presented with an analogue approximation. The algorithms that Kittler so carefully describes that were meant to replicate real-world light phenomena are perversely reversed in order to engender a criticism of the way architects and designers work with digital colour as an instrument rather than an appliqué.

In contrast to physical colour, digital colour is ontologically inseparable from information. In fact, the colour channels and layers that Warburton describes as constituting the exploded image are used more often as a means to transmit information than to produce visual effects. This is particularly evident in the fields of surveillance and behavioural science, where images are both artefacts as well as tools, perhaps even weapons. For those of us in design disciplines, our colour choices, the data we choose to embed in the built environment, can have a wide range of effects beyond aesthetic appeal. Camouflage, augmented reality murals or even the simple QR codes embedded in walls suggest an added dimension or layer to the world around us. As a result, colour can no longer be relegated to discussions of visual effect or cultural meaning, especially in the contexts of digital image production. Working *with* images as opposed to working *on* images, as Koreitem describes, means reflecting on the culture of information processing that surrounds visual disciplines.[8] We can learn from practices that shift or upend our expectations of colour and produce effects that warrant more scrutiny. Double-takes, uncanny imagery, unfamiliar compositions: these are the new tools for piquing interest and diving deeper into what we are looking at.

This expanded consciousness of colour follows a necessary expansion of modes of research and

NEMESTUDIO,
'Four Dioramas', 2021.

criticism into the realm of the techno-social – that feedback loop between technics and social experience that pervades everyday life. If our experience of the world today relies on layers of information processed, and filtered in real-time, we, as designers of the environment, must gain at least some literacy of the technics undergirding this paradigm shift of perception. To this end, questions of what an image is and what an image does require multidisciplinary answers that go far beyond aesthetics. Some maths will be required.

1. Koreitem Z, 'Some notes on making images with computers', e-flux Architecture, July 2019, https://www.e-flux.com/architecture/becoming-digital/248077/some-notes-on-making-images-with-computers (accessed 29 June 2022).
2. Kittler FA, 'Computer graphics: A semi-technical introduction', *Grey Room* 2, Winter 2001, pp 30–45.
3. For a deeper explanation, see Niquille S, 'Regarding the pain of SpotMini, or what a robot's struggle to learn reveals about the built environment', *Architectural Design* 89(1), January/February 2019, pp 85–91.
4. Warburton A, 'RGBFAQ', 27'38" video essay, subtitled, 2020, https://alanwarburton.co.uk (accessed 2022).
5. Joblove GH and Greenberg D, 'Color spaces for computer graphics', in *SIGGRAPH '78: Proceedings of the 5th Annual Conference on Computer Graphics and Interactive Techniques,* August 1978, pp 20–25.
6. It can be further manipulated geometrically to arrive at the cylindrical model of HSL (hue, saturation, lightness), a much more visually accurate form of human colour perception. See Joblove and Greenberg above.
7. Bourke P, 'Generating Hiddenline (wireframe) Images with rendering software', March 1993, paulbourke.net (accessed 25 June 2022).
8. Koreitem, 'Some notes on making images with computers'.

John May and Zeina Koreitem, 'MILLIØNS', Jack Erwin retail space, New York, 2018.

Clouds of Colour

Maya Alam

A/P Practice, AI-assisted recoloration of a 3D scan fragment of *Kliem's Ballrooms*, 2022.

Clouds are complex; so, too, is the subject of colour. Neither can be stably classified, remaining open to continuous reinterpretations. Today, point clouds[1] produced by contemporary imaging technologies might help us look anew at the complicated chromatic entanglements between cultural 'norms', identity and architecture. This essay draws parallels across aesthetics and applications of colour in contemporary female-led design practices by highlighting the potential of so-called 'speculative fabulations'[2] or what I will refer to as 'clouds of colour'. This concept, I will argue, can be deployed to strategically occupy and resist the inherently racist and patriarchal structures of our discipline.

Looming clouds

To locate 'clouds of colour' as a form of opposition, a baseline has to be established on what historically looms in the background for the use of colour in architecture. Often the indexical qualities of chromatic elements in support of the inner compositional logic of a design become sufficient justification for their use: their expressiveness and effect are promptly discarded as 'secondary' and altogether unnecessary. Similarly, due to external circumstances, colour has been leveraged to favour camouflage strategies. If the form of a design is expressive, colour better be absent or used in a diagrammatic manner to create connections between the concept's 'meaning' and its built counterpart. The broader implications behind these strategic uses of colour in design, as they can be found from the Bauhaus to the International Style, might be better understood if we recall Adolf Loos' canonical essay. It is hard to dismiss his closing argument remarking how 'primitive men had to differentiate themselves by various colours, modern man needs his clothes as a mask'.[3] The simplicity and self-assurance of Loos' argument draw a painfully clear line between ideas of a 'modern man', embodied as the cultural ground of his ideological explorations, pitted against a 'primitive man', distant and 'other'. However, what is often considered 'normal' can reveal something more profound about our society and its cultural value systems, particularly concerning social hierarchies and racial supremacy. Therefore, one could argue that Loos was not simply talking about clothing here but a different kind of ideology hinting towards colourism.

The conflation between seemingly universal aesthetics and racist realities has, of course, much earlier origins, as Immanuel Kant's scientific theory of ideal beauty and his introduction of the concept of normal (*Normalidee*) shows. Only if we read Kant's 'Observations on the feeling of the beautiful and sublime'[4] alongside some of his essays like 'On the different races of man'[5] can we understand his contributions as both central to the articulation of German Enlightenment as well as some of the most controversial when it comes to the development of modern racism. Therefore, it is worth acknowledging that some of the origins of these categorical systems originate in (exclusionary) binary thinking, to understand how their biases continue to affect digital culture today.

At the height of the British Empire, painting manuals by art educators standardised the use of 'colour terminology'.[6] One concern was guiding readers in mixing paint to 'correctly' depict skin colours. Oliver Olds' publication *The Trinity of Color, or the Law of Chromatics, or How to Paint* (1892) provides guidelines to mix pigment towards an 'accurate' depiction of what he called 'the trinity of colour':[7] a not-so-subtle subtext constructing a trinity of races, one that normalises the racial identity of his subjects through colour.

Similar strategies were at play when, in the 20th century, continuing practices of colour regulation were embedded in exclusionary thinking in the development of colour photography: this time, it affected the chemical composition of films for still cameras which, targeting a very specific demographic, were explicitly designed to best capture lighter skin tones. In this context, Kodak, one of the leading film manufacturers in North America, established flesh-tone reference cards to calibrate the light sensitivity of its camera film. The Caucasian women in colourful dresses who featured on these cards were commonly referred to as 'Shirley' by men working in the industry from the 1940s up until the 1980s. The 'Shirley card' became synonymous with the entanglements between photographic technological developments, institutional structures and the manufacturing of representation itself through the standardisation and reproduction of skin tone.[8]

Today, in the ubiquitous sphere of digital media in which we operate, the audience for our self-representations extends to include machines and the biases embedded in their software. As a result, contemporary visual culture is shaped by an ever-growing network of image-based activations that break away from the human subject and leverage machine-to-machine communication to articulate what Trevor Paglen calls an 'automation of vision'.[9] This communication is only partially visible to the human eye through RGB values. Too often, repeating well-known tropes of scientific objectivity, we continue to assign ideologies of 'neutrality' to automated processes and mechanisms of vision. However, we cannot divorce the training set from their trainer: the case of Google's 'gorilla' class[10] or Microsoft's Tay[11] demonstrate structural issues that Hito Steyerl refers to as 'Artificial Stupidity'.[12] While we witness an ever-increasing complexity in our cultural landscapes, creating spaces of engagement (i.e. different ways of seeing the world) is imperative. Against this ideological background, and depending on its application, colour becomes both cut and stitch.[13]

Counter clouds

Ibiye Camp

I've been thinking of this gathering, this collecting and reading toward a new analytic, as the wake and wake work, and I am interested in plotting, mapping and collecting the archives of the everyday of Black immanent and imminent death, and in tracking the ways we resist, rupture and disrupt that immanence and imminence aesthetically and materially.

Christina Sharpe, *In the Wake: On Blackness and Being*[14]

British Nigerian multidisciplinary artist Ibiye Camp approaches Sharpe's concept of the wake as a moment of artistic production where the consciousness and possibility of living in the African diaspora meet what she calls 'digital imperialism'. Trained as an architect, Camp uses surveying tools such as photogrammetry to interrogate materials and landscapes, translating them into layered images, videos, Augmented Reality (AR) environments and three-dimensional objects. She notes, 'I use a lot of colour in my work and do not manipulate the scans or RGB values. My interest is in the rawness and fragmental qualities of the mesh.'[15] To her, a scan becomes valuable when it undermines her expectations and rather creates opportunities for further dissection to reveal glitches in the system. This information gap – the space between individual points and their colours that she refers to as 'ripple effects' or 'imprints' – is where she sees the most creative potential.

As highlighted earlier, the 'Shirley card' case is emblematic of the utilisation of colour in the industry of visual representation. This phenomenon still permeates our contemporary understanding of photos and images and led to Camp's commission *Behind Shirley*, created on the occasion of the 5th Istanbul Design Biennial.

During her first experiments with photogrammetry, Camp scanned her own body, only to discover that her hair would not be captured. That voided space (where her hair should be) is where Ibiye recognises one of those ripple effects. From this perspective, her film is a meditation on the biases of software and its related failures. The film begins with a colour scheme emulating 1950s North American aesthetics of 'Shirley cards' to explain itself alongside similar fallacies embedded in surveillance strategies and facial tracking software. To allow viewers to partake in such a charged space of visuality, she developed an application similar to Instagram filters, whereby users could overlay their faces with a low-resolution mask,

From the top:
Ibiye Camp, *Behind Shirley*, 2020.
Ibiye Camp, *Data, the New Black Gold*, 2019.
Ibeye Camp, *Remaining Threads*, 2021.

blending Shirley's colour scheme with the hues retrieved by the facial scan. Updating the composition in real-time, the rapid movements of the viewer's face were programmed to disturb the distribution of the markers deployed by the AR platform to produce misalignments across facial features, allowing the appearance of new colours. If the initial parameters of the 'Shirley card' served as means of exclusion while subscribing to a universal beauty standard, the gaps found in these digital glitches support multivalent narratives of resistance.

The layering of voids, colours, images and timelines is a recurrent theme in Camp's work. Her videos, installations, website and lectures are not developed as singular artefacts. Rather, they exist as layered devices to simultaneously narrate a multiplicity of stories. She explored these forms of visualisation while working on her project *Data, the New Black Gold*. What began as an interest in collapsing timelines, locations and different forms of storytelling has now taken on a life of its own. Her presentations form clouds of colour, allowing the viewers to follow along while simultaneously inserting their associations and narratives.

In her work entitled *Remaining Threads*, Camp combines her digital threading technique with Pelete-bite. Pelete-bite ('pelete' means cut thread and 'bite' means cloth) is a unique craft associated with the Kalabari in Nigeria, whereby fabrics imported from India are altered by pulling threads out of the original textile to produce new intricate patterns. Camp contends that the emerging fabric is quite transparent, so part of the Kalabari tradition is to layer it, sometimes four to six layers, around their waists, mixing colours and taking as much space as possible, and in so doing, challenging Western ideas of beauty. She is interested in leveraging elements of this tradition to speculate on other futures, explaining:

The voids found in the scans are potential in the digital materiality to expose another way of seeing and reading landscape... The technique of Pelete-bite, the way it makes a new condition, a new material as a way of pulling from the voids and the gaps, is similar to how I understand digital space and the question of the voids allowing for renewal – extricate for restitution.[16]

A/P Practice with Lulu Jemimah and Vitjitua Ndjiharine, *Kliem's Ballrooms – Revisited*, 2022, video still.

Maya Alam, Lulu Jemimah and Vitjitua Ndjiharine, performance of *Greetings from Afar*, 2022.

Maya Alam, Lulu Jemimah and Vitjitua Ndjiharine

The practice of Alam/Profeta explores how imaging technologies place points as central elements in the construction of contemporary visual languages – deploying them as spatial coordinates, RGB colour values, UV mapping coordinates and surface intensities. However, rather than accepting the depiction of the point cloud as an obedient representation of a single, monolithic truth, we examine the potential of these clouds as they begin to redirect our focus to the space created in between each surveyed data point. This space most directly accounts for the flickering quality of point clouds as one of the most abstracted forms of visual communication – vaporising wholes into infinitesimal attributes – while simultaneously recuperating old tropes of scientific realism commonly associated with photography.

This expansive interest is articulated across radically different visual registers and becomes a central strand of our research, developed during the 'Dekoloniale' Berlin Residency programme (2022): focusing on memory culture in the city by uncovering and transforming marginalised narratives in Berlin's public space, the project takes inspiration from an almost forgotten theatrical work from the 1930s to highlight the fragmented memory of anticolonial and antiracist resistance fighters. As an expression of diasporic identity combatting racist stereotypes, a group of black German performers wrote and organised the play *Sonnenaufgang im Morgenland* ('Sunrise in Morningland'). Today, the original site of the play, 'Kliems Festsäle' ('Kliem's Ballrooms'), presents itself as a collection of seemingly disconnected fragments. The layered material traces of what once was a series of ballrooms, a theatre, a poultry exhibition space, a military hospital in World War I, a cinema and the legendary dance club 'Cheetah' were carefully documented through photographs and 3D scans.

The resulting data was then used in collaboration with Namibian multimedia artist Vitjitua Ndjiharine to develop a series of visual, spatial and performance-based interventions to empower descendants and related communities of resistance. Ndjiharine's work alters archival photographs by cutting and reassembling and re-presenting to retrieve, in her words, 'silenced voices and counter-histories from the colonial archive'. Her interventions address these discourses on visuality, archival photography and what is discursively explored as the 'colonial gaze'.[17]

Maya Alam and Vitjitua Ndjiharine, 'From Negative Space to Spaces of Resistance', 2022.

Similar strategies were deployed to entangle archival photographic records with scans of the theatre's remains: the black-and-white images were altered with an AI-assisted recolouring procedure, which was in turn layered with manual paint and overlaid with elements of the 3D scans. As Ugandan writer and producer Lulu Jemimah re-enacted the play, entitled *Greetings from Afar*, by stitching together timelines through writing, a series of still and animated interventions provided the visual scenography of the performance.

We found another site for intervention on the grounds of the destroyed Royal Ethnological and Anthropological Museum, now part of the Martin-Gropius-Bau Museum. The museum has faced criticism because it continues to tell the story of Adolf Bastian, its first director, without mentioning the dehumanising colonial practices that his curation supported.[18] Our collaborative intervention, entitled 'From Negative Space to Spaces of Resistance', leverages digitised engravings of the original building to highlight the space of protest located beyond its historical footprint. A large-scale, painterly application of coloured spray chalk on the ground marks the possibility of a new territory, connecting spatial fragments reconfigured from cross sections of the historic building with four 4m-high flags designed by Ndjiharine. The splash of colour in an otherwise grey urban fabric, in combination with the ephemeral quality of the images and materials, flickers between a site of protest and hope.

Folly Feast Lab

It is important for us that as two queer Lebanese women, we are forging a way for the type of work we are interested in doing.[19]

Yara Feghali, a co-founder with Viviane El Kmati of Folly Feast Lab, notes that their work is informed by what Legacy Russell in *Glitch Feminism* would call 'multitudes', creating an aesthetic field of practice that connects their Lebanese roots and queer identities, the cultural milieu in which they operate (Los Angeles) and their immersive gaming environments, demonstrating that 'imbuing digital material with fantasy today is not a retro act of mythologising; it continues as a survival mechanism'.[20] In these environments, colour becomes an essential component of their world-building, supporting emotional responses as well as subtly embedding references to cultural signifiers.

Their project '#TalkAboutBeirut' is a 'reactionary awareness project' motivated by the tragic explosion that occurred in 2020, whereby a massive amount of ammonium nitrate stored at the port of Beirut exploded and destroyed lives, ripping huge holes into the city fabric. As Feghali explains, 'Our only experience of the trauma happening in this place was fictional, delivered to us through media, so we tried and used all the images one could find on social media and online platforms to reconstruct it.'[21] Confronted with the lack of coverage, Feghali and El Kmati began asking friends and family to take photographs that would allow them to reconstruct and document the remains of their city: a participatory photogrammetry archive built at once at a distance and from within. From this perspective, the often-low resolution of the processed point clouds manifests the physical voids left behind by the explosion as much as the fragmented narratives embedded in the collective media archive they built. In opposition to the grey fog that immersed the entire city and desaturated media coverage, the artificial night sky, deliberately chosen as a figurative extension of the saturated buildings' point clouds, creates a dreamlike setting, allowing an imaginary place of memory to persist.

While in a point cloud each point is indexed with an RGB colour value to make the environment visible to the human eye, queer culture has long reclaimed the use of colour as a form of protest and resilience.[22]

For their project 'Be.longing', LA Forum asked five selected architects to work with five authors. Folly Feast Lab partnered with Terry Wolverton, whose personal biography and writings about the Women's Building in Los Angeles were instrumental for the Lesbian Art Project and many other initiatives fighting for LGBTQ+ rights. Feghali recalls her conversations with Wolverton about the latter's arrival in Los Angeles in the 1970s, when she finally felt safe. Feghali says, 'For us, coming from Lebanon… it does not feel like a matter of 50 years ago; it feels very today.'[23]

To portray this experience, Folly Feast Lab tell the story of a fictional character, Amal, which means 'Hope' in Arabic, driving through the streets of Los Angeles in search of safety and her queer community. The proposal's point of departure depicts a fictional community throughout seven Los Angeles neighbourhoods and 37 homes. Their scans are then carefully stitched together, balancing curated moments of continuity with the inherent specificities of each block. From an outsider's perspective, only the rainbow flag symbolises

Folly Feast Lab, 'Be.longing', 2020.

the presence of Amal's community, but for others, many visual cues are interwoven into the fabric of the animation. This results in an immersiveness directly related to one's social and cultural viewpoint. To Feghali, Amal's journey is about finding identity and the longing to belong somewhere.

Folly Feast Lab's work is inherently chromatic – it plays with concepts of beautiful and cute while challenging and recalibrating aesthetics. The work is not concerned with a singular plot line but with a collection of colours, images and atmospheres that tell multiple stories in a nonlinear manner. Drawing inspiration from Shira Chess's 'Play like a feminist' game theory, their digital environments celebrate these multitudes; 'not a beauty, but beauties'. Indeed, colour is never about just one but about many.

When reflecting on the use of colour in architecture, focusing on these clouds of colour might help find design sensibilities beyond the self-affirming determinacy of binary thinking. A clouded territory in between colours can embrace sites of resistance and heterogeneity.[24]

Folly Feast Lab, '#TalkAboutBeirut', 2020.

1 A point cloud, typically created using laser scanning or photogrammetry, is a set of data representing the external 3D shape of a real-world object or scene using many individual dots in a 3D space. Each dot contains information about its position and colour, creating a digital copy.
2 Haraway D, 'Speculative fabulations for technoculture's generations: Taking care of unexpected country', in Kirksey E (ed), *The Multispecies Salon*, New York: Duke University Press, 2014, pp 242–262.
3 Loos A, 'Ornament and crime', in Ward M and Miller B (eds), *Crime and Ornament: The Arts and Popular Culture in the Shadow of Adolf Loos*, Toronto: YYZ Books, 2002, p 36.
4 Kant I, 'Beobachtungen über das Gefühl des Schönen und Erhabenen', first published in 1764, cited in Gray SH, 'Kant's race theory, Forster's counter and the metaphysics of colour', *The Eighteenth Century* 53(4), 2012, p 395–398.
5 Kant I, 'On the different races of man' (first published in 1777 as '*Von den verschiedenen Rassen der Menschen*'), in Eze EC (ed), *Race and the Enlightenment: A Reader*, Oxford: Blackwell Publishers,1997, p 38–49.
6 Bailkin J, 'Indian Yellow: Making and breaking the imperial palette', in Jay M and Ramaswamy S (eds), *Empires of Vision*, New York: Duke University Press, 2014, p 197–203.
7 Olds O, *Trinity of Color, or, The Law of Chromatics, or, How to Paint*, University of Maryland, College Park, MD, 1892, pp 27–29.
8 Roth L, 'Looking at Shirley, the Ultimate Norm: Colour balance, image technologies and cognitive equity', Canadian Journal of Communication 34, 2009, p 113.
9 Paglen T, 'Invisible Images: Your pictures are looking at you', *AD Architectural Design* 89(1), *Machine Landscapes: Architectures of the Anthropocene*, 2019, p 26.
10 Hern A, 'Google's solution to accidental algorithmic racism: Ban gorillas', *The Guardian*, 12 January 2018, https://www.theguardian.com/technology/2018/jan/12/google-racism-ban-gorilla-black-people (accessed 1 June 2022).
11 Megan G, 'Racist in the machine: The disturbing implications of algorithmic bias', World Policy Journal 33(4), 2016, p 111–117.
12 Steyerl H, 'Gott ist doof. On Artificial Stupidity', online lecture, 2017, https://www.hkw.de/en/app/mediathek/audio/55711 (accessed 30 May 2022).
13 Cárdenas M, 'Trans of Color Poetics: Stitching bodies, concepts and algorithms', *Scholar & Feminist Online*, *Traversing Technologies*, 13.3–14.1, 2016, https://sfonline.barnard.edu/traversing-technologies/micha-cardenas-trans-of-color-poetics-stitching-bodies-concepts-and-algorithms (accessed 28 May 2022).
14 Sharpe C, *In the Wake: On Blackness and Being*, Durham: Duke University Press, 2016, p 8.
15 Camp I, in conversation with the author, 13 July 2022.
16 Ibid.
17 Rensing J, 'Ovizire-Somgu: From where do we speak?: Artistic interventions in the Namibian colonial archive (2018–2020)', *Journal of Southern African Studies* 48(1), pp 81–102.
18 Adolf Bastian's curation included the collection of human remains to support pseudoscientific racist anthropological studies. While international debates surrounding the repatriation of body parts of Indigenous people have become more prominent, the only reference to this dark history was a remembrance placard in memory of Bastian's assumed achievements. On 16 November 2022, after the deinstallation of our intervention, an additional information placard was installed.
19 Feghali Y, in conversation with the author, 22 July 2022.
20 Russell L, *Glitch Feminism: A Manifesto*, New York: Verso, 2020, p 24.
21 Feghali Y, in conversation with the author.
22 Nazi Germany used the colour pink in the form of a downward triangle to mark concentration camp prisoners that had been identified as gay men. As a form of reclamation and resistance, this colour symbol became the precursor to the 1978 rainbow flag. See Plant R, *The Pink Triangle: The Nazi War Against Homosexuals*, New York: Henry Holt and Company, 1986.
23 Feghali Y, in conversation with the author.
24 The artists, architects and designers cited in this paper generously donated their time and shared their insights into their projects. I [Maya Alam] would like to thank Ibiye Camp, Yara Feghali, Vitjitua Ndjiharine, Lulu Jemimah, the Dekoloniale-Berlin team and my partner Daniele Profeta.

Prismatic

Marcelyn Gow

Two aesthetics exist: the passive aesthetic of mirrors and the active aesthetic of prisms. Guided by the former, art turns into a copy of the environment's objectivity, or the individual's psychic history. Guided by the latter, art is redeemed, makes the world into its instrument, and forges – beyond spatial and temporal prisons – a personal vision.[1]

Counterposing 'the passive aesthetic of mirrors' to 'the active aesthetic of prisms' in a document outlining the aims of the Ultraism movement in literature, Argentinian writer Jorge Luis Borges and his Ultraist colleagues invite us to consider what a prismatic approach might produce in other forms of art and architecture. The self-declared aim of Ultraism, 'to impose unheard-of features on the universe', could aptly be applied to the architectural and artistic work under consideration here.[2] This selection of projects by educators, architects, digital artists and game designers provides a spectrum of approaches for engaging the prismatic qualities and pedagogical modalities of colour in contemporary architecture.

Prismatic refraction, unlike the mirror's more placid reflection, splits white light into a spectrum of colour that oscillates with vitality. The prismatic spectrum optically transforms the way we apprehend objects in the world, redefining their contours and imbuing them with vibrant materiality. The projects on these pages – all instantiated as public exhibitions in the Southern California Institute of Architecture (SCI-Arc) Gallery in Los Angeles – can be understood through the dichotomy posed by the aforementioned mirror and prism.[3] These exhibitions perform as educational reflections, mirroring aspects of our world and simultaneously reorienting them to be understood anew. This work can also be viewed prismatically as a series of activations that invite us to imagine architecture through a different lens, one that enables architecture and design to engage with a precise spectrum of cultural, technological, social and environmental issues.

In articulating how the work of the Ultraism movement operates in relation to precedent, the authors of the 'Ultra Manifesto' maintain:

The Ultraists have always existed. They are the ones who, ahead of their times, have endowed the world with new aspects and expressions. To them we owe the existence of evolution, which is the vitality of things.[4]

The projects on these pages speak to the vitality described by Borges and his Ultraist contemporaries. These works populate the imagination with contour, radiance and colour. They accentuate spatial orientations and draw our attention to details, thereby proposing myriad ways of imagining and inhabiting the world. Using terms that correspond to various attributes of reflected light – lustre, radiance and brilliance – we can delineate specific modalities of how colour is activated as an architectural material in each project.

Lustre: *n. The quality or condition of shining by reflected light; sheen, refulgence; gloss.*[5]

Pulse is the term selected by Yve-Alain Bois and Rosalind Krauss in their 1997 book *Formless: A User's Guide* to characterise the spatial effects produced by Marcel Duchamp's 'Rotoreliefs: Precision Optics' from 1935. The optical illusion produced by each rotating disc of the 'Rotoreliefs' suggests that the proximity of the viewer to the disc oscillates over time. The act of rotation exerts a visual force that momentarily draws the artwork closer to the viewer before it appears to recede again. The ambition of Bois' and Krauss' volume (and the 1996 exhibition they curated at the Centre Pompidou, Paris: 'L'Informe: Mode d'emploi') was to undo prevalent modernist categorisations within art historical discourse and supplant them with more contemporary ways of critically examining specific works of art. To this end, Krauss and Bois argue that the oscillation of 'Rotoreliefs' challenges 'the modernist exclusion of temporality from the visual field'.[6] Thus, this piece counters the modernist definition of visual artwork as form in stasis and opens the strictures of medium specificity.

Likewise, Florencia Pita & Co's 'Pulse', a colour-driven transformation of the SCI-Arc Gallery, exerts pressure on architectural convention. 'Pulse' explicitly foregrounds the presence of colour, alluding to qualities found in furnishings, interiors and ornamentation rather than aligning with the more familiar material constituents of architecture's palette. Hues of pink and purple in the exhibition conjure an architecture comprised of alternative materials that behave quite differently from the more familiar tectonics of wood, concrete or steel. Colour in 'Pulse' operates with a lustre that is indifferent to gravity and mass. In conjunction with the sinuous formal qualities of the bubble-shaped objects to which it is applied, shades of purple create the illusion that these solid objects are inflated. This effect of buoyant materiality radically alters the notion of Vitruvian *firmitas*[7] in architecture.

Rather than indexing the contours of discrete objects in the space, the pink lustre in 'Pulse' is applied as a continuum that slides through the dimensions of vertical and horizontal surfaces alike. Pink operates prismatically, allowing specific architectural features in the space to become elusive. The edges of adjacent objects dissolve into the glow of colourful light that bounces between them, creating a sense of mystery regarding their extents. 'Pulse' leverages the thinness of manifold acetate sheets to produce filigree structural forms, allowing colour itself to function as the tectonic of the installation. The glossy, pink vinyl flooring and the pink light reflected onto the walls of the gallery imply that colour *is* the architectural surround rather than merely a topical finish.

Strangely incommensurate effects occur. Paper-thin sheets perform tectonically. The glossiness of the tendril objects and the floor surface produce the impression that they are comprised of pools of wet paint rather than solid material. Through its emphatic foregrounding of lustre and colour as fundamental architectural properties, 'Pulse' introduces new conventions into the architectural vocabulary.

This spread: Florencia Pita & Co, 'Pulse', 2006.

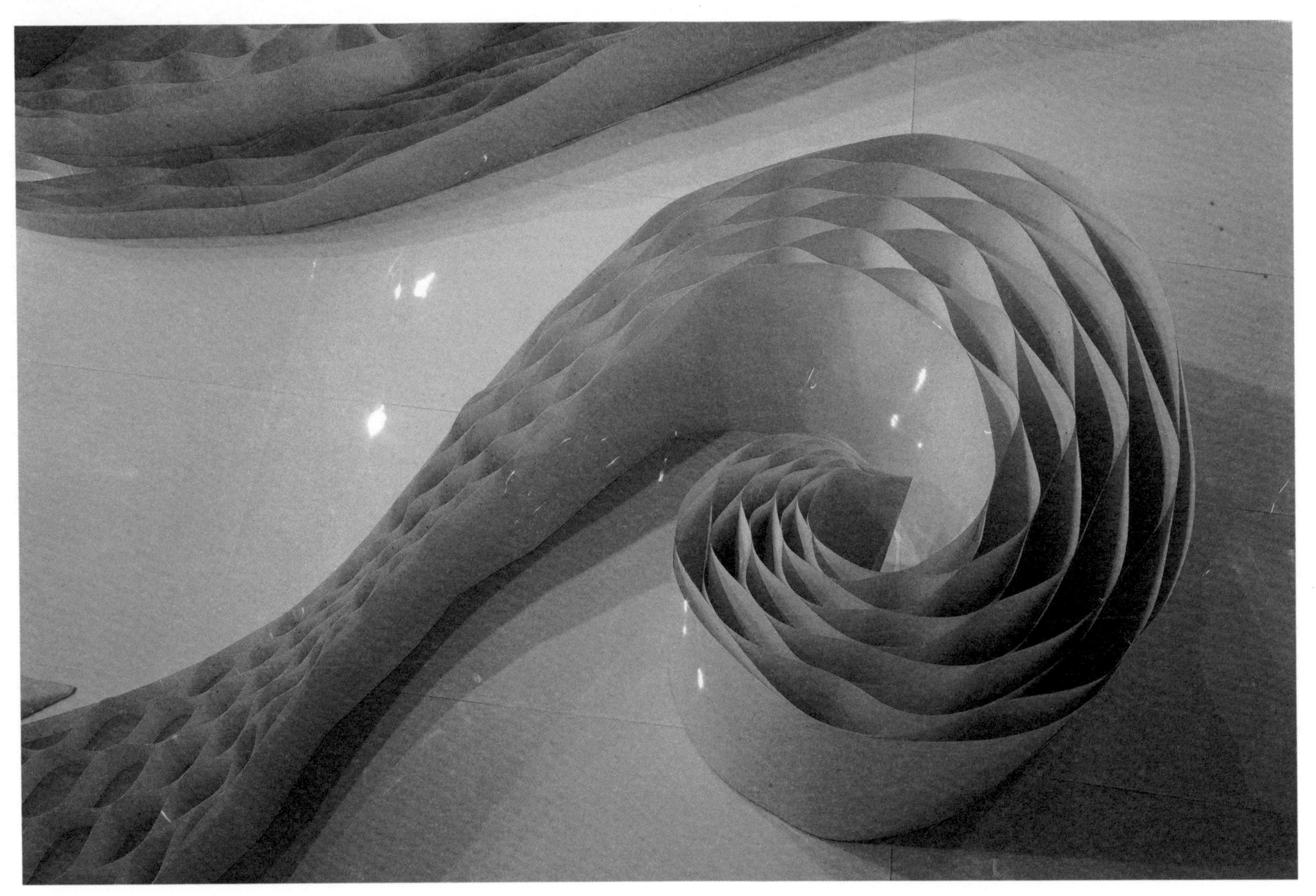

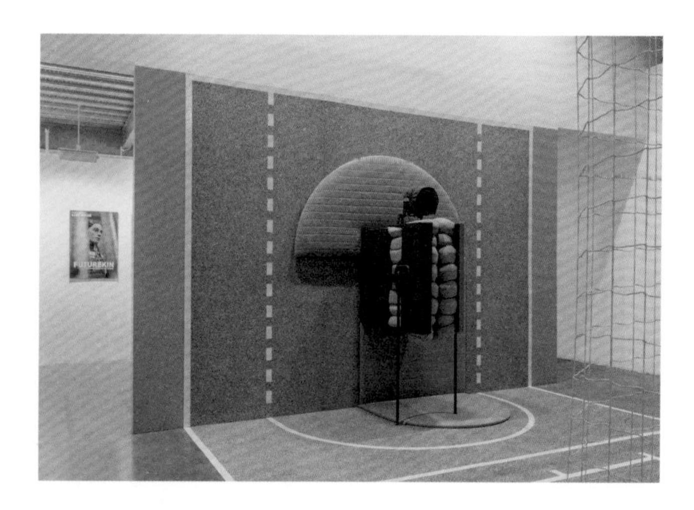

This spread: Lucy McRae, 'Futurekin' exhibition, 2022.

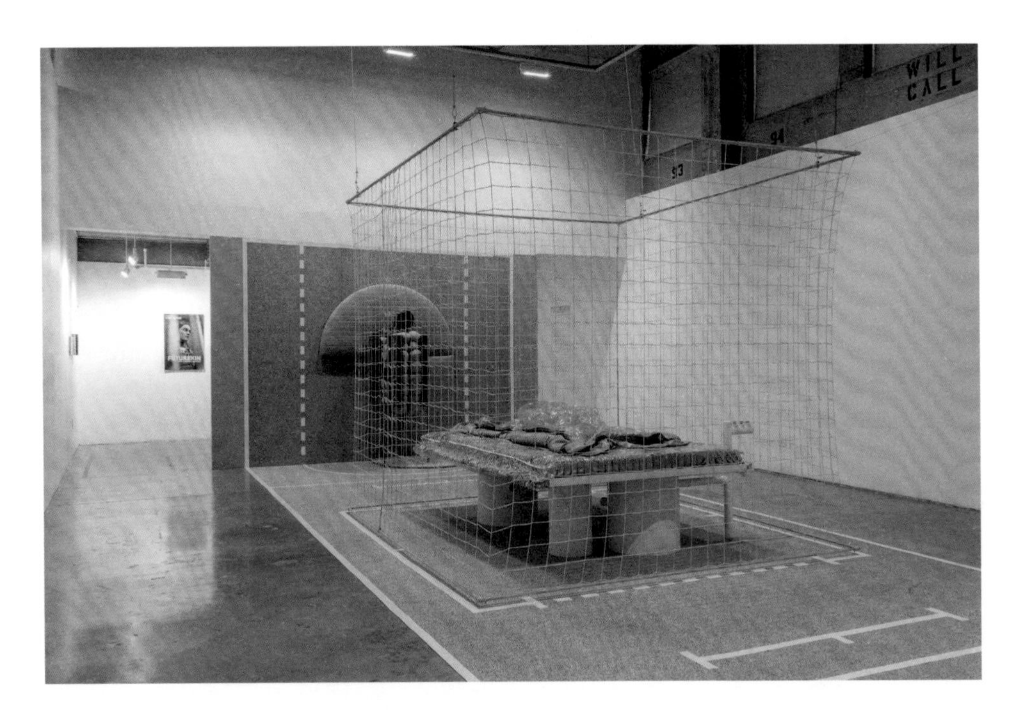

***Radiance:** n. A radiant condition or quality; brightness, light, esp. brilliant or splendid light emitted by an object.*[8]

In Lucy McRae's exhibition 'Futurekin', colour is deployed as a harbinger of possible technological futures. Colour radiates out from the assembled objects in the exhibition, transforming them into multi-coded entities. In the wall text accompanying the exhibition we are told by McRae that these colourful apparatuses, furnishings, garments and equipment belong to a narrative where genetically engineered, future-humans have radically altered sensory capabilities and needs. This set of equipment maintains affinities to the technological, the scientific and the laboratory, yet the objects could also be constituents of sporting events or altered domestic landscapes. The interior assembled here evokes human presence through the scale of the objects relative to the human body, yet it raises questions as to what activities could transpire within the space imagined for technologically modified humans of the future.

In the machines 'Heavy Duty Love, Compression Carpet' and 'Compression Cradle', colour migrates away from familiar sites to produce new readings. The orange and yellow of biohazard warnings, deployed to signal danger, adhere to a series of 'future-sensitive' garments imaged in the installation. These colours alert us to a cautionary view of a biologically transformed future. Other surfaces in the exhibition are materialised in the beige tone of packing tape, creating the impression that they are literally adhesive. This tectonic of taping alludes back to the sports context where taping augments the physical performance of bodies.

The saffron-coloured plastic sheeting of 'Compression Cradle' not only looks as if it could envelop an absent body, but it also performs as a substitute for bodily presence itself. The infusion of colour into the translucent plastic suggests that this sheeting is neither synthetic nor organic. In this guise, colour emits chemical properties that are reminiscent of a laboratory setting. It implies that synthetic materials have been alchemically transformed into organic entities, echoing the proposed biotechnological forms of human care that are the subject of 'Futurekin'.

Each object in the exhibition is staged in a manner that produces multiple readings. 'Compression Cradle' is a furnishing that might be construed as either a bed or a table. The netting making up the perimeter of this furnishing is reminiscent of a cradle textile as well as the netting in a sports arena. Cork-toned flooring wraps vertically to encompass the wall of the exhibition space that performs as the backdrop for 'Compression Carpet'. This vertical folding transforms carpet to wallpaper and suggests that human bodies adopt a variety of physical orientations in the space. This spatial repositioning mirrors the conceptual reorientation we are asked to adopt in a world of biologically modified 'Futurekin'.

***Brilliance:** n. Intense or sparkling brightness or radiance, lustre, splendour.*[9]

Brilliance of colour characterises Damjan Jovanovic and Lidija Kljakovic's 'Discovery: A Story about Rooftops, Airships, Robots and Inflatables'. The exhibition and game take us on a journey through an urban ecosystem inhabited by a hacker community invested in the prospect of reimagining and engineering environmental futures. In this simulated world, virtual renditions of buildings replete with curtain walls, steel, stone and brick act as a backdrop to screens of colour that float slightly in front of the facades of the buildings. Colour here is suffused with qualities of neon signage illuminating the urban scape. The colour's impossible thinness is rendered through a series of colossal graphics that redraw the underlying layers of architectural ornamentation on the facades beneath. This architectural applique differentiates itself from more familiar forms of ornament that index human presence through the size of windows and floor-to-ceiling heights, rather it redraws the building elevations and suggests a more extensive form of urban inhabitation.

In a chapter from *Principles of Art History* dedicated to the role of clarity in Renaissance and Baroque painting, art historian Heinrich Wölfflin describes the shifting relationship between colour and form in painting. According to Wölfflin, 'Colour will not counteract clarity, and yet the more its own life begins to stir, the less it will be able to remain in the service of mere things.'[10] 'Discovery' deploys a colour palette that is animated in the sense described by Wölfflin. The glow and vibrancy of the blue, fuchsia and green hues of 'Discovery' transform colour into a character in the unfolding story of ecological futures. Colour drifts in front of a cityscape reminiscent of previous forms of human habitation, producing a brilliant, new urban figuration.

This spread and next page: Damjan Jovanovic and Lidija Kljakovic, 'Discovery: A Story about Rooftops, Airships, Robots and Inflatables', 2022.

Mirror and prism

The Ultraist distinction between the mirror and the prism underscores two fundamentally different ways of artistically operating in and on the world – one that dwells in the certitude of familiarity and the second that reorients us by opening new avenues for inhabiting the world. The work of the SCI-Arc Gallery exhibitors presented here provocatively upends this dichotomy by working through a combination of the two approaches. 'Pulse', 'Futurekin' and 'Discovery' transform the placid reflections of our surroundings through the optics of the prism. These projects instrumentalise a prismatic approach to colour, reimagining what architecture can do and the multitude of possible futures it can bring into existence.

The biofutures described here are populated by glowing airships, robots and inflatables that adapt conventional architectural elements such as fenestration, panelisation and glazing systems into new typologies for nurturing various forms of life, including humans, vegetation, robots and artificial intelligence. In the game world, the operation of sectioning through hybrid architectural/equipment objects reveals interiors that seem to be comprised of solid striated masses of alternating colour. The striations move across interior surfaces to counter the presence of a fixed ground. In this universe, architecture is rendered as a series of floating entities.

'Discovery' also situates colour as a mode of negotiating the shift from physical to virtual space. Brilliantly coloured airships drift through the virtual urban scape projected into the exhibition space as a form of cinematic gameplay. At certain moments the levitating virtual airships align with the physical inflatable that hovers overhead in the gallery. A continuity of coloration moves from the field of luminous, virtual pixels to the patterned textiles of the inflatable airship and a series of beanbags on the gallery floor, creating the effect of a mirror world existing inside the projection of the game world. The gallery space suddenly opens out far beyond its physical extents to reveal an alternative eco-technological city.

1. Borges JL, Sureda J, Bonanova F and Alomar J, 'Ultra Manifesto', in *On Writing,* trans. Levine SJ, New York: Penguin Press, 2010, p 3.
2. Ibid.
3. The gallery of the Southern California Institute of Architecture (SCI-Arc) operates as an educational platform where SCI-Arc faculty and other guests are asked to develop new work specifically for the gallery. These exhibitions form a significant part of the academic discourse at the school.
4. Borges *et al.*, 'Ultra Manifesto', p 3.
5. 'lustre, n.1', OED Online, December 2022, Oxford: Oxford University Press, https://www-oed-com.sciarc.idm.oclc.org/view/Entry/111401?rskey=uclGpJ&result=1 (accessed 2 January 2023).
6. Bois Y-A and Krauss RE, *Formless: A User's Guide*, New York: Zone Books, 1997, pp 32, 134.
7. *Firmitas* is the Latin word for strong or structurally stable. The Roman architect and engineer Vitruvius listed the term in his treatise *De architectura* as a fundamental quality for building virtuous architecture.
8. 'radiance, n.', OED Online, December 2022, Oxford: Oxford University Press, https://www-oed-com.sciarc.idm.oclc.org/view/Entry/157230?redirectedFrom=radiance (accessed 2 January 2023).
9. 'brilliance, n.', OED Online, December 2022, Oxford: Oxford University Press, https://www-oed-com.sciarc.idm.oclc.org/view/Entry/23334?redirectedFrom=brilliance (accessed 2 January 2023).
10. Wölfflin H, *Principles of Art History: The Problem of the Development of Style in Early Modern Art*, trans. Blower J, Los Angeles: The Getty Research Institute, 2015, p 281.

Colour is a Place as Well as a Thing

Sam Jacob

Sam Jacob Studio, 'Array', Science Museum, London, 2018. An installation in the atrium of the museum formed with coloured cord arranged as rays, forming a spatial effect with vectors of colour.

Architecture is usually understood as a material practice, an act of arranging solid substance into form. These substances are understood in terms of their inherent qualities. We (the cohort of design professionals and consultants typically involved in the production of the built environment) are interested in the way they perform, their strength, their resilience, the way we can shape and form them, their combustibility, their insulating qualities, their cost and so on. Increasingly, we are interested in their provenance and issues around their extraction and production. We think of materials in terms of their inherent qualities, things that emanate from their own internal make-up: the grain they may have, their chemical composition or whatever. That's to say, it's often the physics of a material that is the first concern. Can, we ask, a material perform the job we are assigning it to? A whole system has developed around this, a system that categorises materials in relation to their typical use within building projects. Quantity surveyors can give you square metre rates, engineers can provide rule-of-thumb calculations, and architects might fire up something like the NBS, which in the UK is a specification system that helps articulate material specification within an industry-compliant format. These systems are in place to tame the wild possibilities of materiality, to name and give structure to the complexities outside of professional practice, to define material within a framework and marketplace of commercial building products.

Materiality is also a cultural phenomenon. We ascribe meanings and values to specific material through

Sam Jacob Studio, 'Electric Nemeton', King's Cross, London, 2020. The project combines solid-construction timber structure with layers of fine coloured mesh that form the surface, creating a dialogue between form and structure.

association, traditions and customs or in relation to their cost and scarcity. Ideas of authenticity, honesty and truth are, according to various architectural belief systems, expressed materially. According to these logics, the more substantial the material's presence is, and the more directly its presence is felt, the more substantial are its attributes of authenticity, honesty or truth. Surface appearance is – or rather should be – only a function of the literal depth of construction. Surface as a site itself is rendered suspicious, as a phenomenon that lacks authenticity, behaves mischievously and speaks mistruths. Surface itself – as something distinct from the stuff of building – disrupts the moral structures on which architecture so often claims to rely. The thinness of a surface is read as a lack of moral depth.

There is often a divide between things that are perceived strong and tough, and things that are thin and applied. Maybe it's an attitude that comes out of the patriarchal, military-industrial history of architecture and design. Structure, thickness, weight – things that perform technically belong in one category, decoration and aesthetics are relegated to another. In this categorisation, the thick stuff is serious, the thin stuff less so. 'Inferior design', they used to call it. The physical thinness of decoration is measured as thin in other ways – intellectually, conceptually and morally. It's a problem caused by taking your architectural metaphors literally. It's a problem of applying outdated models of morality (let's say the religious or psychological constructions of our own interiority) to a material world whose way of existing is of an entirely different order.

Clearly the meaning or presence of something isn't measured like that. Presence is presence however – and wherever – it is manifested. And the oppression of surface as a key site of significance is a strangely antithetical idea when we consider that we engage with the material world first through its skin.

Here is a parable about surface, meaning, morality, chromophobia and architecture. The Parthenon Sculptures on display at the British Museum are controversial in many ways: arguments about restoration, ownership, nationalism and the foundational ethics of a museum bound up with the history of empire surround the artefacts. Yet the sculptures themselves are also sites of other ethical questions. First, we understand (and indeed the museum makes clear) that the whiteness of the marble was originally painted. And that the whiteness we associate with classical architecture is a modern myth. A myth so strong that it was folded into the reality of neoclassical architecture. An idealised (and erroneous) idea of the past became the model for the construction of the future. Futures where ideology and meaning were paramount – for example, the architecture of the US Capitol, representing an idea of democracy and suggesting a direct link between classical civilisation and the United States. The surface of the sculptures has another ethical dimension. When Lord Duveen funded the construction of the gallery where the pieces are now displayed, he also demanded that the marbles be cleaned. While the museum's curators denied this request, Duveen went ahead anyway, paying workers to wash them with ammonia and scrape with tools to remove what he considered the surface dirt. In reality, the surface that was removed was the honey-coloured patina of the historical surface. But that patina, understood as dirt by Duveen, was seen as something false, something illegitimate, something that obscured the truth of the materials' interior quality.

Sam Jacob Studio, 'Electric Nemeton', King's Cross, London, 2020. A public installation formed from coloured scaffold net stretched over frames, appropriating the industry standard safety colour-coding of the net as a way to create a more delicate and ethereal presence.

Sam Jacob Studio, Kingly Court, London, 2018. Facade treatment of a historic building in London's Carnaby Street area. The new pattern responds to the physical features of the existing architecture while also suggesting impossible spatial projections.

FAT Architecture, The Villa/Heerlijkheid Hoogvliet, Rotterdam, 2008. A building formed by supergraphics, where colour, text and imagery combine to narrate a reflection on its own local circumstance.

The surface was doubly removed, first colour, then patina. These stories illuminate surface as a highly charged site – a site that may be thin, but a site on which far bigger (and deeper) ideas about culture are played out.

It is not just this prejudice against surface quality per se. It is also, it seems, a desire to exclude the ideas that surface can be articulate about. It is exactly the possibilities of architecture engaging with cultural ideas that is suppressed. Forms of architecture and design that do engage with surface are always in peril of dismissal: the British architecture historian Reyner Banham's description of postmodernism as 'lipstick on a gorilla', for example; or 'Transvestite architecture, Heppelwhite and Chippendale in drag', as Berthold Lubetkin described postmodernism in a 1982 lecture to the RIBA. Both quotes make it clear that the problem with surface is a gendered one, that it is feminine or effeminate; both are also antithetical to 'real' (and masculine or macho) architecture. Both reveal the threat to the established order that surface brings, precisely because it can introduce alternative narratives; precisely because it challenges assumptions about who, what and how architecture might be and who might make it.

Sam Jacob Studio, 'A False Description of the Thing Destroyed', 2016. Speculative reconstitution of an ancient Greek pottery fragment. The pink Fimo clay assumes a form to remake a possible whole, while simultaneously denoting difference.

Sam Jacob Studio, The Cartoon Museum, London, 2018. The interior of the museum projects the graphic space of cartoons into spatial form, where colour and line are used to organise space and create a sense of immersion in graphic space.

It was against this bias that much of FAT Architecture's work operated, under slogans such as 'Taste not space'. The work prioritised the cultural content of architecture and design that we saw as residing in that outer surface: issues of taste, class and value. And in our own way (described as 'aggressive prettification' by Denise Scott Brown[1]) we argued for the potential of all those vilified things – surface, colour, pattern, image – all those things that were usually thought of as unacceptable, beyond the pale, weak or otherwise disregarded. Often, we were designing things with the intention of being provocative and doing the wrong thing deliberately. Another friend described it as an attitude akin to punk's aesthetic of wrapping itself up in the ugliness of culture that surrounded it. But FAT's project – like punk – was finite: perhaps because it was oppositional; perhaps because its project was so well defined, so precise in its area of operation that once fulfilled it was time to move on.

There is another way to figure the problem of surface/material: one that avoids the binary arguments rehearsed above, one that imagines a different relationship and new possibility for the role of the surface.

A note here: 'surface' is a word used in design to talk about the things that are not quite substances themselves. Surface suggests the quality that is carried by a material rather than the material itself. Surface is carried by materials like paints, papers, fabrics, enamels, dyes and coatings, things that manifest properties such as colour hue and tone. These are the things that define the skin of the world around us, and so our direct and most immediate experience of that world.

It's that directness that can also allow us to reformulate the dynamic between material and surface; that can help us recognise that a surface quality itself might even feel material (despite its less-than-material presence).

The qualities that a surface may have are exactly the things that we experience. Surface can feel like a thing, it can appear a space. Though only able to 'inhabit' a surface, qualities such as colour become – or at least appear to become – physical.

Colour is an energy, an aura that projects outwards into space with qualities all of its own, regardless of its host. It becomes something we can touch, a space we experience. Non-materials such as colour become substances themselves.

Once applied, colour becomes a thing. It overrides – or renders irrelevant – the material beneath (who cares if it's really MDF or plasterboard underneath when it's such a beautiful blue?). Colour, in other words, can obliterate tectonics, can merge and fuse assemblies of parts into a singular entity.

Sam Jacob Studio, 'Alternative Instruments', Columbus, Indiana, 2021. A civic sculpture that combines symbols referring to intertwined histories of utopia and colonisation. Colour schemes derived from engineering elements bind these diverse references into a singular urban object.

Sam Jacob Studio, Yinka Ilori Studio, London, 2022. A new studio space for the designer Yinka Ilori. The project developed as a collaboration between the two designers, drawing on their respective design languages of form and colour to define space and mood.

Colour has physical qualities, too. We can feel it, perhaps warm like wood or cold like steel – it is like a material, but also beyond material. A surface rendered in a different colour might feel softer or harder, as if somehow it produced an alchemic transformation of the base it is applied to. Colour becomes material, yet remains immaterial. And in that possibility – of exaggeration, of denial of the material world – colour offers up an imaginative world beyond the metrics and physics of materiality and into other realms of representation and other kinds of sensibility.

An object exceeds its material base and becomes the thing that has been applied to it. The object appears in the world as pink! Or yellow! Or green! It gains properties more associated with cultural fields that are more attuned to colour, with a richer language to describe its phenomena. Fields such as painting, graphic design or fashion are instructive. They can help us believe in the properties of colour as things in and of themselves, to help us recognise the qualities that colours possess, as 'real' and 'authentic' as anything you might find in a builder's yard.

Colour can articulate an object in space, make it feel more present, can separate it from its context, can help define form and shape. Or it can act to weld disparate forms and materials into a single entity. It can assert separation, association or collectivity. If we look, for example, at a painter like Patrick Caufield, we see the ways in which flat colour is used in depictions of interiors. We see how colour choices are made to articulate relationships between objects and space. These choices assert experience and perception as a totality rather than a sum of its parts. So whole areas of wall, furniture and floor might be rendered in a single colour, while a flash of another colour cuts across in a way that might be about light, or about a moment of experience. Colour is used to flatten areas into a background field and then to make present the subject against this field. The spatial logic of the paintings does not simply articulate the constituent pieces, but rather makes a more complex argument about how architectural space is created – not as an assembly diagram but through the ways the parts act together to make the whole.

Colour works spatially too, as a field whose visual energy acts to heighten the sense of objects in space. This field sensation works something like a real-life green screen, as a background that visually isolates and articulates the foreground – the things and people in the space.

Opposite: Sam Jacob Studio, 'Disappear Here', RIBA Architecture Gallery, London, 2018. As part of an exhibition exploring perspectival space, the entrance to the gallery was transformed into an illusionistic space through layers of lightening blue screens. These draw on pre-perspectival techniques used in paintings to create the suggestion of depth.

Below: Sam Jacob Studio, 'Disappear Here', RIBA Architecture Gallery, London, 2018. Perspective drawings from the RIBA drawings collection were hung in relation to each other, their vanishing points forming a cohesive web across the surface of the wall. In turn, the wall was painted to project the space of the room into a representational space according to the same perspectival principles. The installation blurred the relationship between real and representational space.

Sam Jacob Studio, 'A Very Small Part of Architecture', Highgate Cemetery, London, 2016. A framed structure created a 1:1 version of an unbuilt Adolf Loos design for a mausoleum. Colour, translucence and lighting were used to contradict the original design's monumentality, instead rendering it as a ghostly resurrection of a building that never existed.

Think of the thin washes of orange that form the field on which Francis Bacon's horrors of bodies and objects play out. Or the mysterious depths of a Rothko. Or the drippy washes of Hurvin Anderson. These are all fields that are both flat treatments of the canvas and suggestions of depth and space. They remain oscillating between those two states – between the fact of paint-on-canvas and the representational space that the paint-on-canvas creates.

Think, too, of the pre-perspectival technique of early Renaissance painting where distant views are rendered in bands of ever-lightening blue, creating a kind of atmospheric depth. Here, bands of colour are used as if they were stage set flats arranged one behind the other to form a visual sensation (or perhaps code) for depth. Nearness and farness are shown through flat uses of colour. Depth and space are not formed through the mechanics of perspective or foreshortening but through colour itself.

If we understand painting as first representational then material, that's to say, as a world created within the frame and on the flat surface of the canvas, architecture exists in the opposite way. Architecture is the world first. But this shouldn't blind us to the idea that it is also, simultaneously and as much, a representational space. The techniques of, say, Caufield, Bacon, Rothko or Anderson can be folded back into the world so that sensations of space are not only a function of metrics but also of sensation.

Contrast these approaches with Lord Duveen's mania to remove the surface of the Parthenon Sculptures in order to reveal what he supposed was an interior material purity. The possibilities of representational space show us that there is no greater truth contained within. Rather, surface always speaks its own truth, however much we might attempt to scour it away.

Colour is a place as well as a thing. Its use reveals ways of making architecture that connect to wider aesthetic culture. It allows meanings and sensations to be coded into the world. It allows the possibility of architecture to recognise its representational nature. It is, of course, all the things that Lubetkin and Banham suggested it might be. But rather than repress and exclude it, rather than cling to a meagre idea of architectural truth, we should embrace the possibilities of the surface; recognise its significance, its depth and its profound effect on our perception. Indeed, we should reverse Lubetkin's and Banham's complaints, and recognise the more open possibilities of truths that are present in lipstick and drag.

1 In conversation with the author.

When Grass is Not Green: Botanising the Asphalt

Paulette Singley

The Renzo Piano Building Workshop (RPBW), California Academy of Sciences, San Francisco, 2008.

Trees! How ghastly!
Piet Mondrian[1]

After having ingested blue gelatine and cake icing, on 2 November 1996, Jubal Brown, a student from the Ontario College of Art and Design, intentionally vomited onto Piet Mondrian's *Composition in Red, White and Blue* hanging in New York's Museum of Modern Art. This visceral commentary demonstrated the position that he couldn't 'stomach some of the art world's masterpieces'.[2] If only Brown had swallowed green instead. It is well known that Mondrian did not appreciate the colour green. If his Neoplasticist paintings do not sufficiently evidence this, then Charmion von Wiegand's anecdote should: he had such a 'general revulsion against green and growth [that] when seated at a table beside a window through which trees were visible, [he would] persuade someone to switch places'.[3] In a similar but somewhat antipodal story, Robert Venturi changed the colour of his mother's house from light grey to pale green as a cheeky response to Marcel Breuer's advice to avoid green in domestic architecture.[4] All of this goes to say that, for a number of architects and artists, the colour green elicits anxiety.

Known for its high alcohol content and cheap prices, absinthe is a green spirit made from a combination of wormwood, aniseed, fennel and wild marjoram. It became so popular in the 19th century that, as Kassia St Clair recounts, 'Whole districts of Paris were said to smell faintly herbal between 5 and 6pm, a time that became known as *l'heure verte* ("the green hour")'.[5] In the 1980s, it was discovered that the walls of Napoleon's 'damp little room in St Helena were papered with a verdant design containing Scheele's green'[6] (copper arsenite green, an arsenic-laced pigment discovered by Carl Wilhelm Scheele in 1775).

Rather than mawkish green, radical black was to emerge as the preferred colour of the avant-garde, a choice lingering in passé architecture schools that resist exploring sustainable and resilient approaches to building design. In this milieu, green architecture signifies something dowdy, undertheorised, crunchy granola, compositionally awkward or generally embarrassing. Indeed, in *Green Dream* (2010) Winy Maas, co-founder of MVRDV, posits that one of the strongest prejudices to overcome with respect to sustainability is the notion that 'green buildings are ugly'.[7] Moreover, the challenges of greenwashing, that is the veneer of resilience painting over projects that are, in fact, sustainability calamities, introduces the colour of money into any critical discussions on this topic, contributing to an acute understanding that green architecture is freighted with internal contractions of marketing strategies and profit margins.

Berm

Stemming from the Old English grene, in reference to the colour of living plants or grass, green's etymology evokes verdant fields replete with grazing fauns and dancing butterflies. That it has come to represent the colour of hope, life forces and vitality was made explicit during the 1970s environmental movement. Rachel Carson's 1962 publication of *Silent Spring*, exposing the harmful effects of DDT, the 1969 Union Oil Platform spill and the 1973 oil crisis helped spur interest in protecting the planet's ecology. Architecture's response was to go underground and to turn green by constructing earth-berm buildings,[8] implementing photovoltaics, building community gardens and eventually redecorating one's kitchen with avocado-green appliances.

Considered to be the father of modern earth-sheltered buildings, Malcolm Wells pioneered the principle of 'gentle architecture', the goal of which was to 'leave the land no worse than you found it'.[9] After spending 10 years spreading corporate asphalt across America, as Wells states, he changed direction and located his architecture underground. Writing in a 1971 issue of *Architectural Digest*, Wells posited 15 goals to achieve this, including the use and storage of solar energy, recycling waste, providing wildlife habitat and beauty.[10] In his design of 'Solaria', a house for Robert and Nancy Hoffman located in Vincentown, New Jersey, he provided for a three-foot-thick earthen roof and solar collection system in the design of a building that looked like a natural hill covered in wild flowers.

A more recent and perhaps more appealing example of Wells' admonishment to submerge buildings into the landscape is Renzo Piano's California Academy of Sciences in San Francisco's Golden Gate Park (2008). This 37,000m² project houses an aquarium, planetarium, natural history museum and research facility, all gathered under a 2.5-acre living roof. Some 1.7 million native Californian plants, in biodegradable, coconut-fibre containers, grow from an undulating rooftop whose hills and valleys reflect the large, vaulted spaces below and remind visitors of the Sierra Nevada mountains behind. While providing open space for a new wildlife corridor, this earthen blanket of vegetation helps to cool the museum's interior, entirely negating the need for air conditioning on the ground-floor public areas and research offices along the facade. As Piano explains, insofar as 'the green roof with its bubbles is like foliage wrapping itself over branches', the building is made of arboreal 'shadows'.[11]

Grass

Emerging as the largest irrigated crop in the United States, one that renders the front and backyards of countless suburban landscapes green, is the lawn – showcased in cultural phenomena such as *The Lawnmower Man* (1992) and the 1999 Canadian Centre for Architecture exhibition publication *The American Lawn*. Besides consuming vast amounts of water, the lawn's monoculture creates biological wastelands, contributes to stormwater runoff, relies on chemicals to thrive and requires massive amounts of petrol to mow.[12] While the decorative green lawn slowly gives way to more functional gravel, mulch, drought tolerant landscapes or edible gardens, it remains a stubborn dream of English estates, ha-has and pastoral animals. The biggest challenge with the lawn, however, is that it is thirsty.

As scientists measure the effects of climate change with increasing precision, they identify paradoxes and anomalies in micro-environments around the world that offer clues for understanding that growing plants is not always the right strategy to make the earth green. In an essay titled 'Earth gets greener as globe gets hotter', Tia Ghose reports that 'leafy green vegetation has increased dramatically over the last several decades, thanks to excess carbon emissions'.[13] According to satellite data collected by NASA's Moderate Resolution Imaging Spectroradiometer (MODIS) sensors and the National Oceanic and

A sea of greenhouses, stretching for tens of kilometres, surrounding the town of El Ejido in the Almería province of southern Spain. The image was acquired on 20 July 2008 by NASA/GSFC/METI/ERSDAC/JAROS and US/Japan ASTER Science Team using the Advanced Spaceborne Thermal Emission and Reflection Radiometer (ASTER).

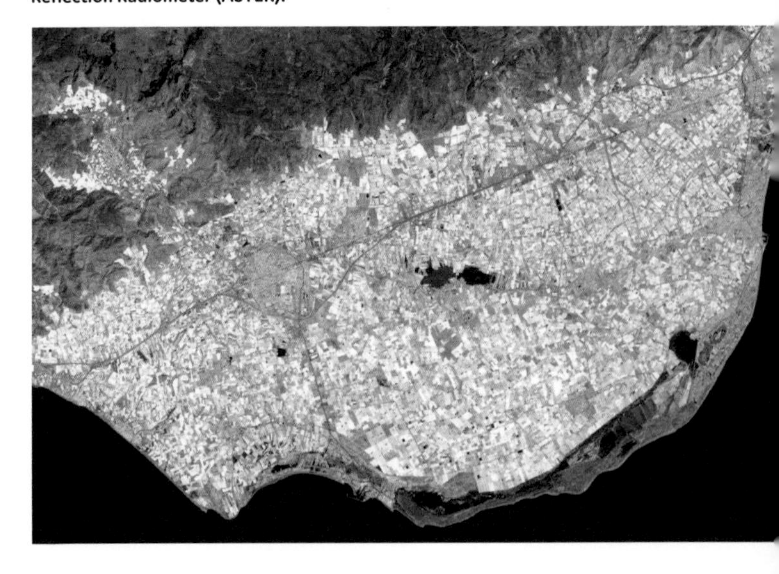

Atmospheric Administration's Advanced Very High Resolution Radiometer instruments, scientists concluded that about 70% of the greening could be attributed to increased atmospheric CO_2 concentrations that augment photosynthesis.

Another NASA report considers transformations in Almería, Spain, where an estimated 150 square miles of greenhouses can be found to have merged into a continuous white plastic canopy. Known in Spanish as *inverdaderos*, these greenhouses contribute 2.5 to 3.5 million tons of fruits and vegetables per year, making Almería an important source of off-season tomatoes, peppers, cucumbers and melons.[14] Basing their conclusions once again on observations from NASA's MODIS sensors, researchers at the University of Almería have calculated that the greenhouses' high reflectivity contributes to increasing the area's surface albedo, resulting in a cooling effect of 0.3°C (0.5°F) per decade between 1983 and 2006. This positive turn, conversely, relies on the negative twist of depleting Almería's water table by an annual water deficit of 170 cubic hectometres.[15]

A similar story about feeding the world whatever and whenever it wants afflicts Peru's Ica Valley, where the large-scale production of asparagus has drained the area of its water. Given that the asparagus grown in this desert climate requires constant irrigation, the local water table has significantly dropped, in some places as much as 8m each year.[16] In an age when agriculture consumes approximately 70% of the world's freshwater, we enjoy the benefits of 'virtual water', a commodity transported from one place to another via so-called green vegetables.[17]

Mound

Winy Maas coined the phrase 'green dip' as a way of expressing MVRDV's goal to cover the planet with sustainable design.[18] The practice conceived of their project at the Marble Arch Mound, commissioned by Westminster City Council to promote shopping in central London, to showcase this philosophy.[19] A proper English folly, formed by a 25m-tall artificial hill out of which were to have grown lush plants and trees, visitors were asked to pay for the opportunity to climb a staircase, at the top of which they would enjoy views of the pavilion itself, Marble Arch and central London. But just before the July opening in 2021, an unexpected dry spell in London left the plants and trees brown and sparse, rendering the mound an eyesore and was widely ridiculed in a country whose contribution

MVRDV, Marble Arch Mound, London, 2021–2022, photographed on 29 July 2021.

MVRDV, Netherlands Pavilion, Expo 2000, Hannover, 2000. Photographed by Piet Niemann in 2020.

A vertical arboriculturist hanging off the Bosco Verticale in Milan, designed by Stefano Boeri Architetti in 2014.

to landscape gardening significantly influenced the contrivance of picturesque gardens. Immediately after this, the exhibition was closed, tickets were refunded and the blaming began, with client and architect pointing fingers at each other for the botched job. (The mound reopened in August 2021, without an entrance charge, and closed permanently in January 2022.) Instead of providing the built expression of a green manifesto, the sad brown hill reminded us that nature's sublime power for wreckage all too frequently eclipses human attempts to create order. Rather than a failure in the more local sense, however, this project serves as a powerful global bellwether of climate change's impact on locations like London, places we typically tend to imagine as safely cool, wet and green.

A parallel narrative to the story of Marble Arch Mound's demise is MVRDV's Netherlands Pavilion for the 2000 World Expo in Hannover, designed to 'showcase a country making the most out of limited space'.[20] A symbol of sustainable design, the pavilion featured six independent Dutch ecosystems stacked inside the floors of a structural frame that ultimately was left to decay after the World Fair closed. After more than 20 years of abandonment, MVRDV is now slated to transform this cultural ruin into co-working spaces, with two new buildings wrapping around to provide an open interstitial area. They also intend to reconstruct the original third-floor forest. More than focusing on a way to make the planet green, the valuable lesson of this project is its potential happy ending, where abandonment gives way to *regeneration* – a more precise term than *green* or even *resilient* when it comes to architecture's response to natural environments and the adaptive reuse of building resources.

MVRDV's green experiments have resulted in more successful projects. Their Tainan Spring in Taiwan (2020) and Skygarden in South Korea (2017) stand out for offering unique strategies for regenerating decaying urban infrastructure. In the Taiwan project, they excavated a shopping mall's parking structure, transforming it into a public wading pool or metaphoric lagoon. In South Korea, they followed the important model Diller Scofidio + Renfro (in collaboration with James Corner Field Operations and Piet Oudolf) established at the High Line in New York, transforming an old highway overpass into a public garden. While it is possible to hold these projects under a microscope and identify flaws or miscalculations in their carbon footprints, the efforts of municipalities and architects to introduce lagoons into previously flooded brownfield sites or to transform abandoned infrastructure into a pedestrian path moves past the reductive slogan of 'green dip'.

Forest

A highly debated and simultaneously iconic green project is Stefano Boeri's Bosco Verticale (Vertical Forest, 2014) located in Milan, Italy. Mondrian would have had to close the blinds in the apartments of these two residential towers (110m and 76m tall) because they feature 900 cherry, olive and oak trees, along with 5,000 shrubs and 11,000 floral plants, growing out from cantilevered concrete balconies. The design therefore boasts a living green building envelope that provides habitats for diverse species, including birds, insects and humans. The green envelope can extract as much as 14 tons of CO_2 annually from the city's polluted air, while contributing nine tons of oxygen to its atmosphere. The facade-integrated vegetation reduces direct solar radiation during the summer, allows light to penetrate during the winter, mitigates wind forces, releases humidity into the air, absorbs small pollution particles and dampens urban noise – offering the same ecological advantages as 10,000m² of forest. It also purportedly works as a stopgap to sprawl, with each tower offering the equivalent of about 50,000m² of single-family houses.

Additionally, 500m² of solar panels, the use of geothermal energy, the filtered reuse of the building's greywater to irrigate the vegetation and the monitoring of plants' dryness with a digitally controlled probe system are some of the eco-innovations that these buildings contain. Boeri's firm collaborated with expert horticulturalists, botanists and the engineering office of Arup in their design of the 1.1m-deep planting containers that are built to withstand the intense lateral forces high winds transfer onto the trees and ultimately the structure. Finally, one of the more innovative or perilous features are the flying arboriculturists who prune the vegetation while suspended in the air from mountaineering equipment.

And yet, from out of all these remarkable innovations some basic questions emerge. How does the increased weight of the balconies – needed to support the trees and requiring large quantities of carbon-intensive concrete, steel and reinforcement – justify calling this project green? If the trees must be transported to the site and craned up, then how, too, is this a sustainable idea? And, with an irrigation system complicated not only by the sheer amount of water and fertiliser required to nourish the plants but also by the quantity of pipes and pumps lifting it up the height of the tower, how much of a carbon footprint does this system leave? Lloyd Alter summarises a number of critics who suspiciously view the Bosco Verticale as 'green-wrapping': 'It might take those trees a thousand years to pay back the carbon debt of the planters they sit in.'[21]

Daniel Barber and Erin Putalik also question the global trend of 'treescraping', asking whether a mechanised natural system is still a forest? For Barber and Putalik: 'If the forest is a mechanical system, is it still a forest? Can we ask of architecture a capacity to move beyond conceptions of nature as system and resource?'[22] In a profession where trees are being leveraged in the service of rhetorical manoeuvres, they contend, 'The architectural challenge – the global cultural challenge – is to imagine living with a forest that somehow exceeds both nostalgia and instrumentality.'[23]

While these observations carry weight, it is important to consider the significance of this project, if only for focusing world attention on the potential for architecture to respond to climate change and be beautiful. The World Green Building Council refers to the Bosco Verticale as 'arguably one of the most recognisable buildings of the last decade', while Boeri has emerged as 'perhaps the most famous name in green architecture'.[24] The project has been replicated all over the world: Diller Scofidio + Renfro at Pirelli 39 (Milan, Italy), Foster and Partners at Marina Tower (Agios Kosmas, Greece), Thomas Heatherwick at Eden (Singapore), Kengo Kuma at Park Habitat (San Jose, US), MVDRV at Green Villa (Sint-Michielsgate, the Netherlands), Jean Nouvel at One Central Park (Sydney, Australia) and Koichi Takada at Urban Forest (Brisbane, Australia). If Boeri has transformed vertical forests into big business, then he has also developed an important prototype that can be refined and reinterpreted with smaller carbon footprints, such as with his most recent innovations of using mass timber framing and larger, hollow concrete balconies. That he unveiled his Vertical Forest Towers for Dubai in 2022, a desert city where water is desalinated to keep plants alive, lends increased significance to the queries listed above.

Garden

When considering the machine–nature, artifice–sincerity or resilience–resistance dyads, we might look to François Roche, Stéphanie Lavaux and Jean Navarro of R&Sie(n), pronounced 'heresy' in French, with an approach to green that in fact approaches black. Rather than as an instrumental tool or nostalgic memory of an idyllic past, in response to Barber and Putalik's earlier prompt, R&Sie(n)'s work foregrounds a more agonistic approach to nature. Their Mosquito Bottleneck House, an unbuilt design for a client who lives in Trinidad, aspires to a strange cohabitation with an insect that now inhabits the Caribbean: West Nile Fever-infecting mosquitoes. Using the geometry of a Klein bottle, a closed, non-orientable surface that has no inside or outside, the architects elected to accept (in theory), rather than reject, mosquitoes in a space that ultimately pushes them outside without ever penetrating the interior.[25] In this system, 'Exterior surfaces invert to become interior walls and interior volumes intertwine but do not intersect…, mosquitoes can enter the home and live in close proximity to the owner without actually sharing his space, all the while buzzing in a soothing, therapeutic manner.'[26]

With 'I'm Lost in Paris' (2008), R&Sie(n) embraces green-wrapping with exuberance, surrounding a 1,300m^2 residence with 1,200 hydroponic ferns fed by a mixture of bacteria, nutrients and rainwater, and contained in 300 handblown glass beakers. The architects postulate that the neighbourhood is both attracted by the 'green aspect and repulsed by the brewage and the process to produce it'.[27] Attraction and repulsion, machines in the garden and the enemy within all trope the architect's position regarding green architecture that begins to form something of a response to the open questions. Roche understands that nature is both beautiful and brutal. To simply use nature as passive décor, as Roche states, 'is a kind of domination through domestication'.[28]

Walter Benjamin describes the 19th-century Parisian *Flâneur*, a gentleman who strolled leisurely about the city, as 'Botanising the asphalt'.[29] I like to think of this phrase as describing moments when weeds push through cracks in the pavement and giant tree roots take over the sidewalks. This is a world akin to the transformation of Angkor Wat in Cambodia, where strangler figs, kapok and banyan trees have overgrown the Ta Prohm temple. We therefore should recall that buildings with plants growing on them date

Opposite : R&Sie(n), François Roche, Stéphanie Lavaux, Jean Navarro, 'I'm Lost in Paris', 2008.

Right: R&Sie(n), François Roche, Stéphanie Lavaux, Jean Navarro, Mosquito Bottleneck House, Trinidad (unbuilt), 2002.

Below: Ta Prohm temple, Angkor Wat, Cambodia, late 12th and early 13th centuries.

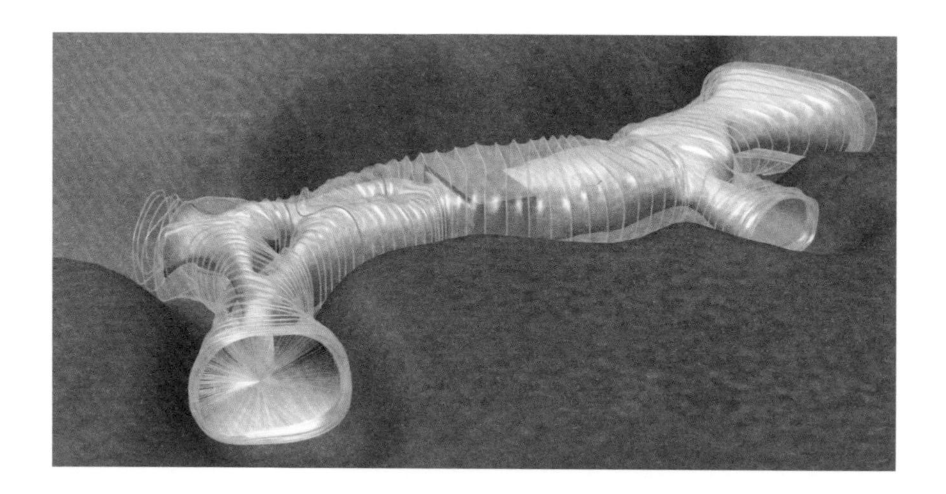

back to the Hanging Gardens of Babylon and dwell in more recent examples of autochthonous sustainable architecture from around the world, such as at the Torre Guinigi in Lucca, Italy, dating from the 1300s, where Holm Oaks grow from the rooftop of this tower, from a site that once served as a kitchen garden.

If green architecture has become a false signifier of resilience, one that masks capitalist enterprises, then perhaps we are better off aspiring to the colour of desert tan instead of watering plants growing where they don't belong? This all having been said, I leave you with these two thoughts: 'Soylent Green is People' and 'It's not easy bein' green.'[30]

Torre Guinigi, Lucca, Italy, 14th century.

1 Knudsen M, 'Mondrian, the city and the birth of Abstract art', *Hypocrite Reader* 3, April 2011, https://hypocritereader.com/3/mondrian (accessed 5 December 2022).
2 Associated Press, 'Art Student "Projects" His Opinions', *Spokesman,* December 1996, https://www.spokesman.com/stories/1996/dec/01/art-student-projects-his-opinions (accessed 5 December 2022).
3 Knudsen M, 'Mondrian, the city and the birth of Abstract art'.
4 Michelle Chang, 'Something vague', *Log* 44, autumn 2018, pp 103–113.
5 St Clair K, *The Secret Lives of Colour*, New York: Penguin Books, 2017, p 217.
6 Ibid, p 224.
7 Maas W *et al*., *Green Dream: How Future Cities Can Outsmart Nature*, Rotterdam: NAi, 2010, p 18.
8 A bermed house may be built above grade or partially below grade, with earth covering one or more walls. See https://www.energy.gov/energysaver/efficient-earth-sheltered-homes (accessed 12 February 2023).
9 Weber B, 'Malcolm Wells, 83, advocate for "gentle architecture"', *New York Times,* 7 December 2009, http://archive.boston.com/bostonglobe/obituaries/articles/2009/12/07/malcolm_wells_83_advocate_for_gentle_architecture (accessed 5 December 2022).
10 Weber B, 'Malcolm Wells, 83, advocate for "gentle architecture"'.
11 Glancey J, 'Second nature', *The Guardian*, 3 November 2008, https://www.theguardian.com/artanddesign/2008/nov/03/renzo-piano-green-architecture-environment (accessed 5 December 2022).
12 Ecosystem Gardner, 'Why lawns are not sustainable in ecosystem gardening', *Ecosystem Gardening*, December 2022, https://www.ecosystemgardening.com/why-lawns-are-not-sustainable-in-conservation-gardening.html (accessed 5 December 2022).
13 Ghose T, 'Earth gets greener as globe gets hotter', *Yahoo,* 28 April 2016, https://www.yahoo.com/lifestyle/earth-gets-greener-globe-gets-hotter-121156415.html (accessed 5 December 2022).
14 'A greenhouse effect has cooled the climate of Almería', *Geography Fieldwork*, https://geographyfieldwork.com/AlmeriaClimateChange.htm (accessed 5 December 2022).
15 Voiland A, 'Almería's sea of greenhouses', *Earth Observatory,* May 2022, https://earthobservatory.nasa.gov/images/150070/almerias-sea-of-greenhouses (accessed 5 December 2022).
16 Lawrence F, 'How Peru's wells are being sucked dry by British love of asparagus', *The Guardian,* 15 September 2010, https://www.theguardian.com/environment/2010/sep/15/peru-asparagus-british-wells (accessed 5 December 2022).
17 'Food companies fail to address water risks in Peru', *Swedwatch,* 13 November 2018, https://swedwatch.org/publication/food-companies-fail-to-address-water-risks-in-peru (accessed 5 December 2022).
18 Fairs M, '"It would be wonderful to design more planets", says Winy Maas', 29 June 2020, https://www.dezeen.com/2020/06/29/design-more-planets-winy-maas-mvrdv (accessed 5 December 2022).
19 MVRDV, 'Marble Arch Mound', https://www.mvrdv.nl/projects/456/marble-arch-mound (accessed 5 December 2022).
20 MVRDV, 'Expo 2000', https://www.mvrdv.nl/projects/158/expo-2000 (accessed 5 December 2022) and Wang L, 'MVRDV plans to sustainably repurpose the Dutch Expo 2000 Pavilion', *Inhabitat,* 11 August 2020, https://inhabitat.com/mvrdv-plans-to-sustainably-repurpose-the-dutch-expo-2000-pavilion (accessed 5 December 2022).
21 Alter L, 'Another look at Stefano Boeri's Vertical Forest', *Treehugger*, 13 August 2020, https://www.treehugger.com/another-look-stefano-boeris-vertical-forest-4859164 (accessed 5 December 2022) and De Chant T, 'More reasons to stop putting trees on skyscrapers', *Per Square Mile*, April 2013, https://persquaremile.com/2013/04/23/there-are-better-ways-to-plant-more-trees (accessed 5 December 2022).
22 Barber D and Putalik E, 'Forest, tower, city: Rethinking the green machine aesthetic', *Harvard Design Magazine*, https://www.harvarddesignmagazine.org/issues/45/forest-tower-city-rethinking-the-green-machine-aesthetic (accessed 5 December 2022).
23 Ibid.
24 Lubell S, 'How Milan's Bosco Verticale has changed the way designers think about sustainable design', *Architectural Digest*, 3 November 2020, https://www.architecturaldigest.com/story/how-milans-bosco-verticale-has-changed-the-way-designers-think-about-sustainable-design (accessed 5 December 2022).
25 Weisstein EW, 'Klein Bottle', *Mathworld*, https://mathworld.wolfram.com/KleinBottle.html (accessed 5 December 2022).
26 'Book Review – Bioreboot: The Architecture of R&Sie(n)', *We Make Money Not Art*, March 2010, https://we-make-money-not-art.com/book_review_bioreboot_the_arch (accessed 5 December 2022).
27 R&Sie(n), 'I'm Lost in Paris', *New Territories*, 2009, https://www.new-territories.com/lostinparis.htm (accessed 5 December 2022).
28 Turpin E, 'Matters of fabulation: On the construction of realities in the Anthropocene', *Architecture in the Anthropocene: Encounters Among Design, Deep Time, Science and Philosophy*, May 2013, https://quod.lib.umich.edu/o/ohp/12527215.0001.001/1:22/–architecture-in-the-anthropocene-encounters-among-design (accessed 5 December 2022).
29 Benjamin W, *Charles Baudelaire: A Lyric Poet in the Era of High Capitalism*, trans. Zohn H, London; New York: Verso, 1973, p 36.
30 From the 1973 film *Soylent Green* and from *Sesame Street*, 'Kermit's Song'.

PROFILE

Working with Colour

Louisa Hutton

In many ways, working with colour is similar to making music. A colour palette can be used in countless combinations to create every possible kind of expression, just as any musical concept can be achieved through the careful synthesis of particular tones and rhythms. Yet the mere application of colour does not automatically yield a worthwhile result: similarly, a mindless mix of tones is also likely to be just noise, its elevation to music is dependent upon the intelligence of the compositional arrangement, as well, of course, as its execution.

While it may generally be considered acceptable to apply colour to non-essential, movable or easily replaceable building parts, the use of colour on structural elements of architecture is still viewed as a transgression: a column treated with polychromy supposedly undermines the very essence of tectonic principles – columns should not only carry the loads of a building, they must also reveal its structural rationale. On a painted column we see various architectural positions coincide: structure versus dressing, conceptual versus experiential space. What if these polarities didn't have to represent *either-or*, but could be regarded as *both-and*? Why not embrace the richness inherent in contradiction, inviting the viewer to engage?

Our interest in the textile in architecture stems not only from our study of Gottfried Semper's observations – it also comes from the understanding that ever since the discovery of the curtain wall, the facade has been released from its load-bearing role, now being responsible purely for spatial enclosure, climatic control and identity. The metaphor of the textile seems wholly appropriate, as, in our view, the facade resembles a dressing. With the idea of dressing another association arises: as in the social sphere, a building must behave in a way that is appropriate to its company. The dress shows respect for its surroundings at the same time that it expresses its wearer's identity. Moreover, there is a similarity between textiles and facades in the endless variations on a theme that in each case is defined by the limits of technology: just as the technique of weaving has not changed over centuries despite variations in thread, looms, pattern and dyestuffs, almost all facades, compositional differences notwithstanding, are still made in a more-or-less similar way. When – through the use of texture and colour – facades finally acquire an almost textile-like appearance, the metaphor is able to be transformed into an architectonic leitmotiv.

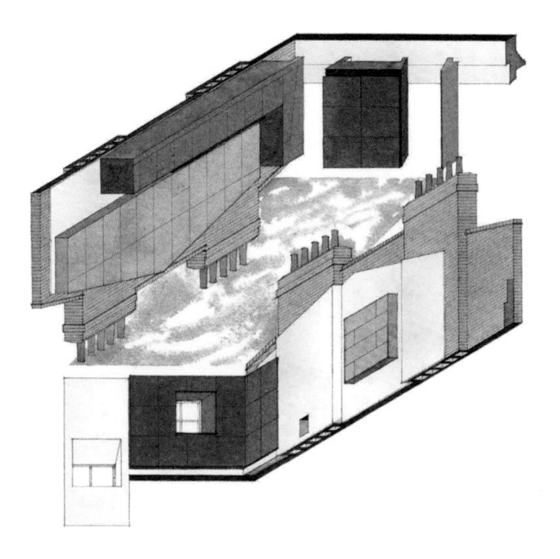

Opposite: Sauerbruch Hutton, 'City Dress', installation for the British Pavilion, 2006 Venice Biennale.

Top right: Sauerbruch Hutton, L House, London, 1992.

Right: Sauerbruch Hutton, H House, London, 1995.

Three London Houses

In the early 1990s we experimented with colour on three London terraced houses in order to optically transcend the narrowness of their spaces. In this we were inspired by the work of Josef Albers, who made a significant contribution to the conceptualisation of colour in modern painting. What we find particularly interesting in Albers' writings such as *The Interaction of Colour* and his life-long series of paintings, *Homage to the Square*, is the realm that lies between the visual space created by the painting and the physical space that surrounds it, which he refers to as *actual fact* and *factual fact* respectively. One could say that we are trying to bring back into palpable space what Albers was achieving on canvas: analogous to the perceptive oscillation that occurs between the *actual* and the *factual* in Albers' paintings, we work deliberately with the alternating perception of three-dimensional space and two-dimensional image. Just as coloured areas juxtaposed with one another can create a *Farbraum* – or illusionary coloured space – so coloured planes or volumes set against each other in real space can make the latter appear two-dimensional, as the visitor becomes engaged in an experience that oscillates between the visual and the corporeal.

Right: Sauerbruch Hutton, L House, London, 1992. Coloured volumes containing the paraphernalia of everyday life allow uncluttered existence with the sky.

Left and opposite: Sauerbruch Hutton, H House, London, 1995. Material and chromatic re-evaluation of a 1960s villa enables gratitude for the luxuriance of nature and space.

M9 Museum District, Venice-Mestre

We are, of course, aware of the significance of colour with regard to its potential within both the immediate and wider physical context of a piece of architecture, or a piece of the city.

This heterogeneous group of buildings forms the Museum District in Mestre, located in a central area of the city that had formerly been in military use and so closed-off to the public for over a century. A new diagonal route from the southeast to the northwest of the site – passing through the courtyard of an old convent – forms the backbone of the scheme, while an east–west way of somewhat smaller scale gives further porosity to the urban tissue. The convent, restored and adapted for new uses, is complemented by a pair of new buildings for the museum that line the diagonal route. A further pair of small concrete structures completes the ensemble, replicating the volumes of two dilapidated stables that, accommodating the cavalry's horses, had been put up some decades previously against the western boundary wall. The five-building ensemble is complemented by two existing structures on the northeast corner of the lot – the former church of the convent, Santa Maria delle Grazie, which had been converted to a cultural centre in recent decades, and a post-war office building.

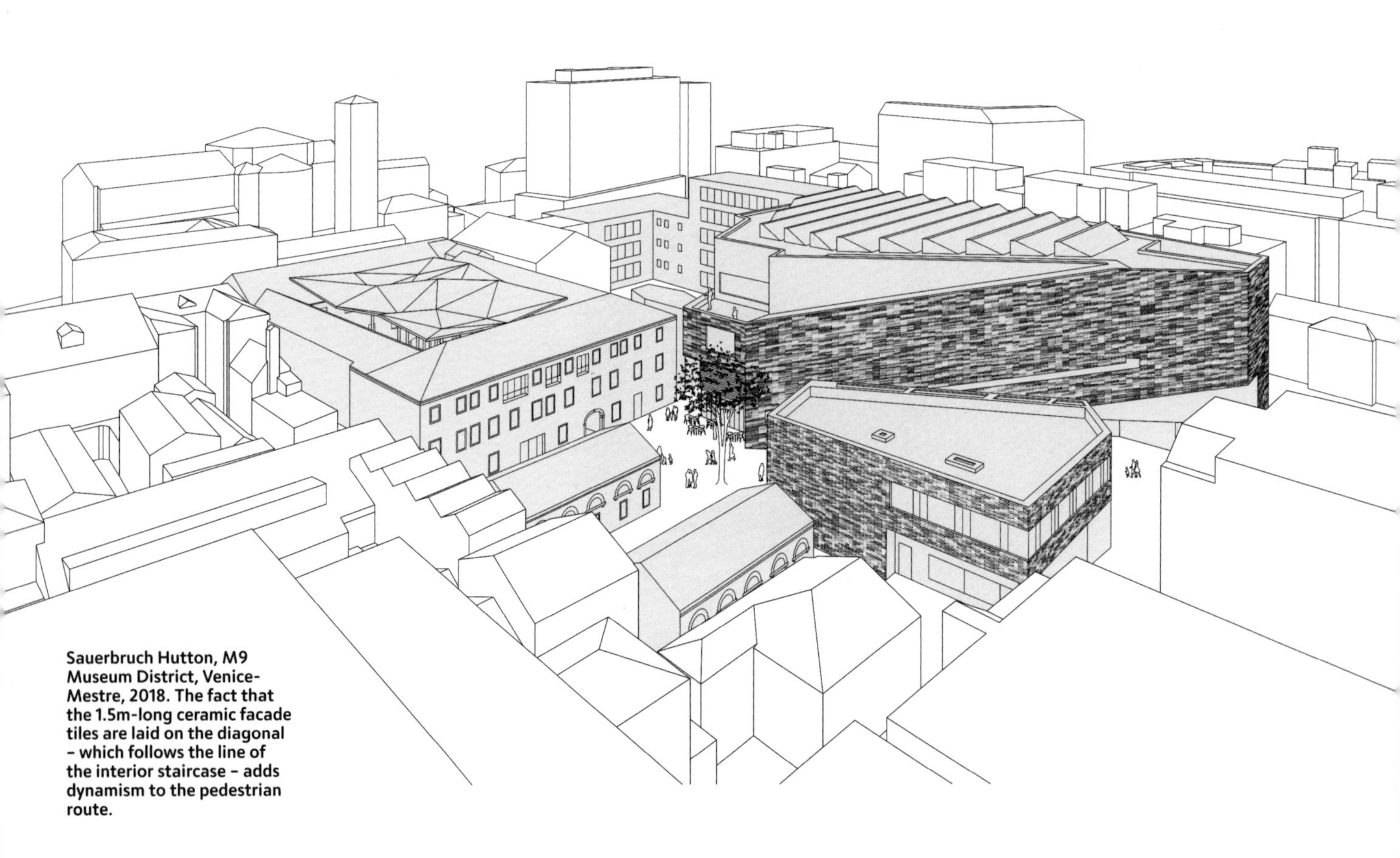

Sauerbruch Hutton, M9 Museum District, Venice-Mestre, 2018. The fact that the 1.5m-long ceramic facade tiles are laid on the diagonal – which follows the line of the interior staircase – adds dynamism to the pedestrian route.

Above: Sauerbruch Hutton, M9 Museum District, Venice-Mestre, Italy, 2018.

Below: Sauerbruch Hutton, M9 Museum District, Venice-Mestre, 2018. The top floor of the museum is differentiated in its materiality (concrete) to help the museum adopt the scale of its neighbourhood. The final selection of hues for the ceramic skin was derived from consideration of its surroundings.

Spreading the functions of the museum over two distinct structures meant that we could somewhat reduce the scale of the new insertion: further reduction resulted from the use of two materials on the larger building such that the upper areas are clad in concrete, while the lower body, in coloured ceramic, builds a strong chromatic relationship with its neighbouring street, the via Brenta Vecchia. While the colour palette of a family of reds, greys and neutral tones was selected to blend in with the surroundings, the form of the new buildings, as well as the scale of their ceramic tiles (that varies between the larger and the smaller structure) announces the M9 Museum of the 20th Century as a clearly new insertion into the fabric of the city. The Museum District brings new life to the city of Mestre, thanks to its many public uses, such as a Saturday market in the former convent's covered courtyard, the new Piazzetta in the heart of the scheme, the many public facilities in the museum's transparent ground floor areas and its generous outreach programme.

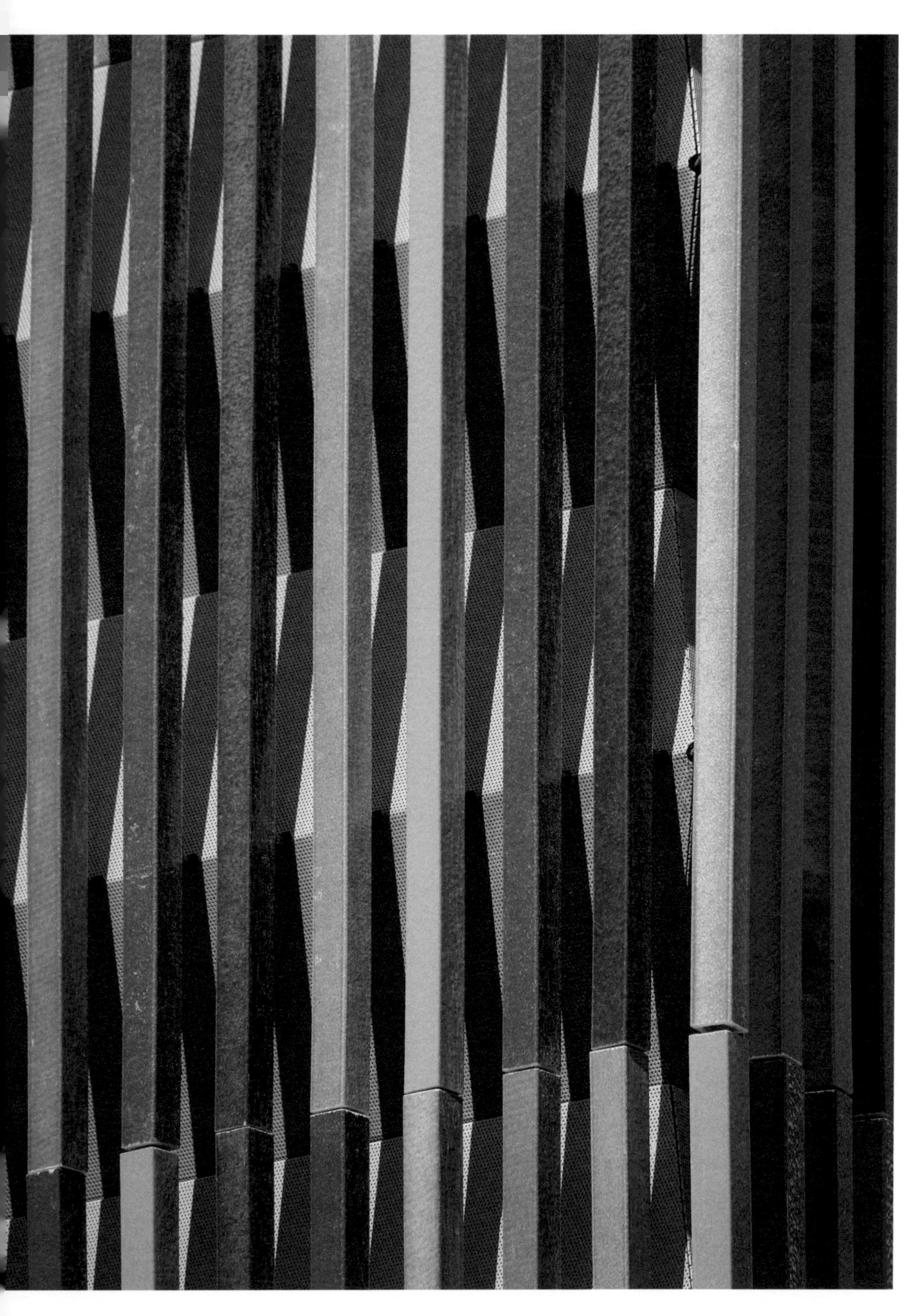

Sauerbruch Hutton, Brandhorst Museum facade detail, Munich, 2009. From close by, the origin of the facade's various rhythms and patterns are revealed to result from a simple combination of vertically hung, glazed ceramic batons and a horizontally folded, bi-coloured metal rainscreen. Of the 23 individual hues of the batons, some arise from the same glaze being applied to differently coloured clays.

Brandhorst Museum, Munich

Colour can be used as a kinetic instrument. One's perception of a building, or the space around it, can be affected by the movement of the observer.

This museum was designed to house a private art collection comprising mostly mid to late 20th-century European and American paintings, with an emphasis on special collections of Andy Warhol and Cy Twombly. As most of the works were therefore generally to be hung on walls – with zenith-quality daylighting on the ground and parts of the lower as well as the upper floors – the exterior facades of the museum were to have very few windows. In contrast to the monolithic appearance of the neighbouring, and significantly larger, all-concrete Pinakothek der Moderne, we realised that it would be important both to optically reduce the apparent mass of the long building and to provide some kind of small-scale variation within its facades. Further, there was an unusual requirement from the city that the building

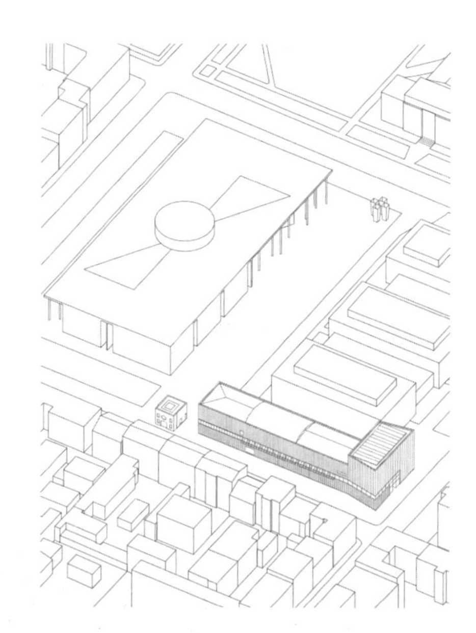

Above: Sauerbruch Hutton, Brandhorst Museum, Munich, 2009.

Sauerbruch Hutton, Brandhorst Museum, Munich, 2009. In order to appear less massive, the museum is optically divided into three: a paler 'head' houses the entrance, foyer and Cy Twombly's Lepanto Room above, while along the street middle and darker tones provide the articulation.

Sauerbruch Hutton, Brandhorst Museum, Munich, 2009.

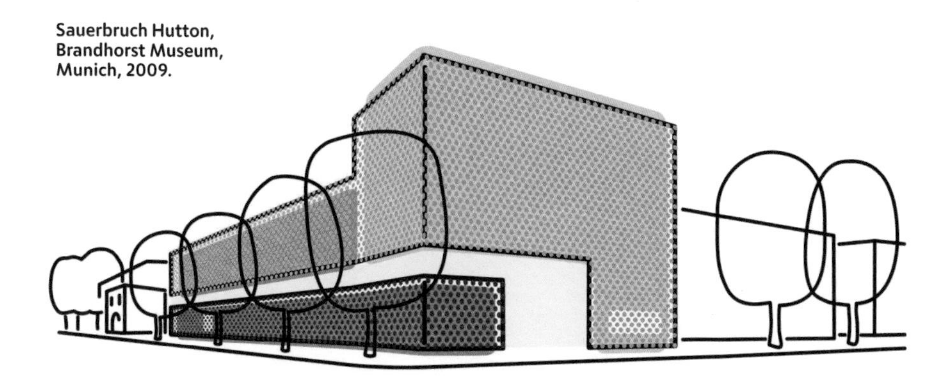

itself should function as a sound-absorbent body with regard to neighbouring traffic noise. In consideration of the fact that in the early 20th century within the realm of painting colour had disengaged itself from form, we decided that an appropriate dress for this particular museum could be a polychromatic coat.

We reduced the mass by optically articulating the building into three apparent volumes, each of differing tonality: the palest being the 'head', which, situated at the street crossing, is a somewhat taller trapezoidal form that contains the entrance, as well Cy Twombly's famous 12-painting sequence of the battle of Lepanto above, while the upper and ground floors of the museum's main wing are each clothed in mid and darker tones respectively.

A first layer of horizontally folded metal provides the rain screen. Perforated on the ground floor areas with sound-absorbent felt mounted behind, this significantly dampens the sound of passing traffic. In front, suspended vertically with gaps providing passage for the street noise, 36,000 4cm-wide glazed ceramic batons form the outer layer of the building.

While from afar the Brandhorst Museum reads as three interconnected, tonally differentiated interlocking volumes, the closer one gets the more these two distinct layers both reveal and combine themselves, such that a view directly onto the facade clearly shows the (bi-coloured) horizontal folds, while in an anamorphic or sideways view the vertical striations of the multicoloured ceramic cladding dominate.

Further, one's understanding of the architecture develops from a perception that, at a distance, is purely optical – somewhat analogous to seeing a screened image – to a distinctly corporeal sensation as, approaching closer, one begins to become almost physically entangled with the building. Right up against it, what had been seen as solid seems now virtually immaterial as elements start to oscillate in varying syncopations of colour and rhythm, and one's body begins to swing.

Opposite: Sauerbruch Hutton, Brandhorst Museum, Munich, 2009. When viewed head on, the dominance of the batons tends to 'give way' (in varying degrees according to their respective hues and those of the rear layer) to the horizontality of the folded metal screen behind.

Below: Sauerbruch Hutton, Brandhorst Museum facade, Munich, 2009. As the building is viewed increasingly anamorphically, the front layer of glazed ceramic batons optically run together until they are all one can perceive.

PROFILE

Colour is a Sufficient Material

fala

fala, 155, House Within a Structure, Gaia, Portugal, 2022–.

fala, 125, House with an Inverted Roof, Guifões, Portugal, 2020–2023.

At fala, we often work with given spaces and existing dimensions. Painting everything in white (also a colour) is a first step in all our projects. White erases mistakes and imperfections, it creates an abstract background for the work to unfold. Then, colourful elements begin to occupy the imperfect white canvases – volumes, rooms, facades. It is worth revisiting fala's early experiments with colour, which we thought radical at the time. From the green kitchen in Apartment in Príncipe Real (016, 2014), to the blue doors and shutters in Apartment in Chiado (025, 2015), to the light blue curtains of the Garage House (040, 2016) and the first pink handrails in the House with Four Columns (059, 2018), to exuberant patterns, and to fully painted facades and ceilings. Glossy green floors are deployed as unifying planes. Doors tend to be distinguished from the walls. Complexities and juxtapositions are favoured. Even exterior volumes are broken surface by surface. It has to do with understanding projects as approximations of elements and systems. Each system is assigned a material or a colour. Green columns in different rooms and levels are then understood as layers among others in space.

The majority of our surfaces used to be painted in white; floors were wood, and colours – if any – would be less saturated and rather minimal. It was a gradual move from furniture to small elements, from elements to extensive surfaces. We developed our use of colour until it became free and natural.

fala, 079, Suspended House, Porto, 2017–2020, interior.

fala, 079, Suspended House, Porto, 2017–2020, rear facade.

For a private commission in Porto that we nicknamed the Suspended House (079, 2017–2020), we began with blue – a relatively easy kind of colour that could conveniently be called 'cold grey'. It then went off to shades of light green. Then pink popped up, a lighter hue that was introduced to bring warmth, and to balance out cold glossy marble pavements. There is a semi-defined palette of colours that repeats between projects, yet it inevitably expands. Blue gets tiresome, pink becomes predictable, new actors constantly enter the scene. Some tones and shades naturally emerge from references – warm yellows recall Gio Ponti's striped ceilings, earthy red facades are reminiscent of Peter Märkli's Haus Kuehnis in Trübbach, Switzerland, and vivid green is inspired by Aldo Rossi's I-beams. The office joke about never using orange, purple or brown remains appropriate.

The Suspended House is actually not very chromatic. The interior walls are predictably white, so are the cabinets. The floor has a chessboard pattern of white and black marble. Its interior is rather sober; the only subtly coloured surface is its light blue ceiling on every level. The centre of the house is punctuated by a suspended concrete column of a complex outline that is accompanied by a set of four dark blue doors on two levels. Nonetheless, the house is not monochrome. Colour finds its way on the outside through banality and repetition; red, green and blue roller blinds are sourced from a catalogue. If open, they disappear. But when fully closed, their colours animate the back facade and project vivid shadows onto its stiff interiors.

A coat of paint is no less important than stone, wood or metal. It is also the most economical. Its amount and intensity often depend on the client. Some clients are open to experimentation, others are fixed on white, grey, beige and brown. In one of his interviews, Rem Koolhaas encourages architects to explore a new world where beige is not a necessity: 'I don't find it troubling per se. In certain situations, I have actually learned to like it. But I find it difficult to feel any enthusiasm for it. I simply feel a slight disappointment that the final aesthetic consensus of humanity is gravitating toward beige.'[1]

Houses are meant to be warm and cosy. In this sense, Waves of Glass and Clouds of Metal (097, 2018–2021) is barely a house. It might as well be an office or an art gallery. To solve a typologically challenging space, two curved walls of glass brick were introduced as devices to separate private from public and allow for maximum light. Two glimmering surfaces run between light blue ceiling and an endless carpet of white tiles. The resulting space is reflective and gleaming. Tiles, glass brick and blue define a crisp canvas that is then populated by small-scale interventions and elements. A protruding staircase becomes a red triangle that is a glorified mistake. Splashes of red can highlight necessary exceptions and happy accidents.

fala, 097, Waves of Glass and Clouds of Metal, Porto, 2018–2021. Protruding staircase.

fala, 097, Waves of Glass and Clouds of Metal, Porto, 2018–2021. Rear facade, detail of coloured metal mesh.

Two red columns anchor both elevations, and a couple of red frames contrast with glass brick. Black often suggests emphasis, and dots and lines of black marble appear throughout the project. A zebra-striped kitchen makes its presence known within the living space. Alongside door handles and skirtings, wood beams framing the triangular opening are perhaps the only hints of conventional domesticity. Otherwise, the material palette dissolves any traditional definitions of 'house'.

The project is organised along a longitudinal axis bracketed by two metal masks: while the rear facade constitutes layers of glass, mirror, metal cut-outs, repeated patterns and fiddly pink handrails, the front facade reads as a misty mass of clouds.

fala, 114, House Within a Few Lines, Porto, 2020–2022. Rear facade.

fala, 114, House Within a Few Lines, Porto, 2020–2022. Light hitting the coloured ceiling.

We don't paint enough walls in colour. And when we do, it is often a complete element or object that gets painted. In the case of the House within a Few Lines (114, 2020–2022), the space is divided and disassembled by colour – columns are green, beams are reddish, ceilings are light blue – our way of creating a reassuring consistency within a complex project. Nonetheless, you could say that it is tediously systematic; groups of elements are properly distinguished, hierarchies are established. Colour becomes an indispensable compositional device.

The geometric challenge of a narrow house such as this one is settled within a few lines. The main space unfolds between two surfaces – a bright turquoise field of ceramic tiles and a light green tented ceiling – all concealed by a corrugated metal roof. The large opening that makes up the rear facade is composed of a concrete beam, a freestanding blue column and a bright shade that can transform the whole room yellow. The side wall of an adjacent building is painted in green. A few stripes of black marble frame doors and windows. A couple of mirrors disguise unwanted thicknesses and chimneys, but also generate perplexing reflections. Here, a concise volume disguises a complex spectacle of interior spaces.

Colour also requires precision. NCS coding and RAL palettes, matt or glossy, texture or no texture, endless 3D renders with 50 options. Often it is sourced from a catalogue, where one can choose between 20 shades of plaster, 15 of which are variations on beige and grey. This is the case with most catalogues: some shade of beige and grey. And brown.

fala, 136, Dim Cloud, Matosinhos, Portugal, 2021.

The brief for an office renovation nicknamed Dim Cloud (136, 2021) meant reinventing an otherwise bland space. We demolished partitions and peeled back layers of plaster from the concrete columns. We then introduced two convoluted surfaces: one a dividing wall, and the other a new ceiling. The complex intersection of these two elements was carefully measured and calibrated. Bathrooms, storage and a kitchenette find their place behind stepped surfaces. Bright blue and light yellow doors are proudly present, while the floor is proudly cheap. The short sides of the stepped wall are highlighted in black. Joints between bathroom tiles are yellow. The blue wavy ceiling is populated by an even grid of downlights, suggesting references from another time and place. Beams of light are reflected on a multitude of broken surfaces. The resulting space gleams and reverberates.

Over the course of our practice, colour has become a celebrated norm. Its application is extended over more and more surfaces. Its meaning is questioned and challenged from project to project. Maybe white will appear less and less present. Maybe we'll break our own rule and paint a wall in orange. Colour is a joyful tool and a trope of sorts that persists. Can architects not be considered joyful colourists? To quote Ettore Sottsass, 'Colours are like words. With colours you can tell stories. Words have histories and stories and significances within themselves. For example, "love" means one thing, but "amore" in Italian means something else, slightly different... Colours are the same.'[2]

Our commitment to colour is now so strong that photographs of our projects in black and white seem wrong. Yet, discoveries are still to be made and unexpected tones are to be applied. Perhaps blue and green are to be abandoned. When it comes to colour, we are interested in breaking our self-imposed limitations.

Colour is both logical and intuitive. It brings elements together and separates them from the neutral background. It brings character to space, acts across various scales and becomes a defining feature in some projects. It facilitates formal readings. It contrasts. It dissimilates. Colour is easy. Colour is contested (in fact it doesn't always survive competitions or client meetings), but things are getting better in this regard; colour is quickly overcoming its reputation as unnecessary decoration. Indeed, it has become a spatial element, such that projects are assembled out of figures, lines and colours. In short, colour is a sufficient material.

1 Boehme J, 'Interview with Rem Koolhaas', *The Believer* 121, 31 January 2020.
2 'There is a Planet', Triennale di Milano exhibition, curated by Barbara Radice, 2017.

PROFILE
Notes on the Velocity of Colours
David Batchelor

These days many of our cities are both Kansas and Munchkinland: by day, landscapes of monumental greyness formed in concrete, steel and glass, or in the muted colours of the earth, in stone and brick; by night, luminous theatres of hyperkinetic colours that cascade out of billboards and neon signs and LED screens and bounce off every reflective surface and spill onto the streets below.

If this is true of our cities, or at least some parts of them – some areas, some streets, some buildings – then I want to ask about the mechanics of this relationship between a city's architecture and its colours. Many of the more nocturnal colours of buildings are, obviously, bolted on after the event. Or, more specifically, the engines of these colours are usually attached to buildings in the form of signage, advertisements and decoration of one kind or another. For the most part, I am fine with this relationship. Grey buildings make good supports for illuminated colours, be those colours of advertisements or, more occasionally, artworks. Shiny surfaces distribute those colours in cascades of luminosity that drench the streets below.

This is not a novel observation. Nearly a century ago, Walter Benjamin, the great analyst of the city and of colour, summed it up in two sentences when he asked: 'What, in the end, makes advertisements so superior to criticism?' And answered: 'Not what the moving red neon sign says, but the fiery pool reflecting in the asphalt.'[1] There is so much in this self-depreciating observation. Advertisements are superior not for what the sign may say, but for what we might see – in this case, the dance of coloured light in a pool of water on a dark asphalt road in the city at night – and Benjamin was always alert to the mute eloquence of colour.

A discussion of architecture and colour is always a discussion about degrees and types of colour, not about its presence or absence. There is, obviously, no such thing as a colourless building, even if that building is a glass box or a whited sepulchre. Colourless architecture

David Batchelor, 'Sixty Minute Spectrum', programmed LEDs, 2017.

may have been a fantasy among certain modernists, a fantasy that may in turn have been perpetuated through black-and-white photography, but, to my mind, the principal difference is really between the intrinsic colours of materials and various forms of applied colour. And within the broad arena of applied colour, the biggest difference is between the largely tonal and the emphatically chromatic.

This, for me, is where the relationship becomes more difficult and, at the same time, possibly, more interesting. With a few very significant exceptions, such as the dwellings of Luis Barragán, colourful buildings, in which vivid colour is or feels somehow integral to the structure, do not seem to me to work very well, or at all. At best the colours look arbitrary, or self-conscious, or an afterthought. At worst, they just look wrong and I wish they weren't there. For some time, I have wondered why this is.

I don't think the problem lies with some underdeveloped chromatic ability among architects (although sometimes I do wonder). And, equally, I don't think the problem is solved by bringing an artist on board to advise on better colour choices (although sometimes I wouldn't mind). I have come to think the problem of architecture and vivid colour, if that is what it is, lies elsewhere. I have begun to think the issue is related to what I will call, only because I can't think of a better way of phrasing it, the different temporalities of colour and architecture.

Contrary to what our brains constantly try to persuade us, colour is not a property of objects, colour does not inhabit materials, colour is not fixed to surfaces, because colour is not securely attached to anything at all. Or, if colour is attached to anything, it is to another thing that is itself not a thing: light. If colour is, in almost all cases, an effect of light, then it is more useful to think of colour as an event, as something that happens under specific conditions, and when those conditions change or cease, colour changes or ceases. Colour, then, is always transitory. In spite of the neurological illusion of colour constancy, and in spite of our technological attempts to make it endure, colour is fleeting, it resists stasis, and it doesn't respond well to being pinned down. Colour, to misapply the words of Charles Baudelaire, the great 19th-century poet of the modern city, is 'fugitive', it is 'ephemeral' and it is 'contingent'.[2] And the more vivid the colour, the more fugitive it appears to be.

I know rather more about colour than architecture, but buildings appear to me to be much slower things. And the bigger they are, the slower they tend to be. (This sounds rather obvious, perhaps too obvious, but bear with me, I'm not from these parts.) Architecture tends towards the monumental: the solid and the stable, the enduring and the permanent. Even when it aspires to something more fluid and futuristic, architecture tends to dramatise rather than to shed these associations. Buildings, big buildings in particular, are slow structures, and these slow structures don't chime with the quickness of colour. Colour resists stasis; you might also say: colour resists structure. Which is to say, the temporality of architecture is more or less the opposite of that of colour. And this may be one of the reasons why colour and architecture have such a fraught relationship. Vivid colour is always unsuited to and uncomfortable in conditions that imply permanence and fixity. This might be one reason why I find it a lot easier, and a lot more pleasurable, to imagine a brightly coloured beach hut than a brightly coloured office block.

This is not in any way to suggest that vivid colour and architecture should be kept apart. On the contrary, and as I suggested above, there are innumerable examples of dynamic encounters between buildings and colours. Rather, colour, being mobile and impermanent, is better combined with architecture in ways that preserve these characteristics. The question then is how can buildings present colours in ways that don't conflict with the basic characteristics of colour? And, vice versa, how can colours coexist with buildings in ways that don't conflict with the basic characteristics of architecture?

There are many architectural traditions that combine vivid colour with enduring structures. Stained-glass windows are the most obvious and dramatic examples of this relationship. Likewise, mosaics and glazed ceramic tiling of one kind or another can cover just about every internal or external surface of a building, and the same can be said of frescoes made in wet plaster. Any or all of these forms of colour may last for centuries, and they may have been designed and executed with a single part of a single building in mind, and they may be physically inseparable from that building. But in an important sense they are not of the building; they are not integral to its fabric; they could always be removed, at least in the imagination; they are conceptually independent of the structure.

And that, for me, can be the basis for a rich and lasting relationship. The different temporalities can coexist quite happily, so long as they retain a level of independence from one another. And beyond that, perhaps, colour and architecture might simultaneously offer contrary compensations. The compensations of colour: momentary delight in the surfaces of the impermanent. The compensations of architecture: the illusion of stability beneath these surfaces.

Sixty Minute Spectrum

It was with rather more inchoate versions of these notions in mind that in 2017 I proposed a treatment for the restored skylights on the newly refurbished Hayward Gallery in London. The 2m-tall glass pyramids – there are grids of 36 and 48 units across the two roof-spaces – are a highly visible feature of the flat-roofed building. My proposal involved programming an LED lighting system fitted inside the pyramids so that at any one time they all glowed the same vibrant colour. However, over the course of an hour, the colour moved very gradually through the visible spectrum. On the hour the pyramids glowed red; over the course of the next 60 minutes, the colour shifted, almost imperceptibly, like the minute hand of a watch or clock, through purple to blue to green, to yellow and orange and back to red. Titled 'Sixty Minute Spectrum', the installation functioned (if you knew how to read it) as a rudimentary clock. Less an attempt to slow down colour, perhaps, than an attempt to slow down the process of looking at colour, it has been reinstalled at the South Bank Centre each winter since 2017.

In broad brush terms, 'Sixty Minute Spectrum' is just a very large example of a type of work I have been making in the studio for some time. In a 30-year attempt to make colour the centre and subject of my two- and three-dimensional work – to make colour vividly present as itself, to make colour a noun rather than an adjective – I have often found myself placing vibrant coloured forms on simple neutral supports. This, I have come to realise, can have the effect of isolating colour from its surroundings and identifying colour as the focus of the work.

David Batchelor, 'Sixty Minute Spectrum', programmed LEDs, 2017.

David Batchelor,
***Concreto, 6.0/01*, 2019.**
Glass and concrete.

Concretos

In each work from the group collectively titled *Concretos* (2012–), a vividly coloured element of one kind or another is set into a simple rectangular concrete base.[3] The first of these were inspired by the universal deterrent mechanism that consists of sticking shards of coloured glass into the cement tops of medium-height walls.

Since then, I have tried applying this simple process to a wide range of different materials and objects. A few years ago, as I was moving studios, I stumbled across a box of old coloured plexiglass offcuts from an abandoned project. I began to embed some of these fragments in concrete bases; and then to place them in clusters of overlapping transparent colours. *Reef* (2016) comprised over 30 individual elements in a kind of diorama of perforated transparent colour. To some they resembled a highly artificial coral-like structure, to others they suggested an abstract chromatic cityscape.

At the time of writing, I am still looking for the limits of the *Concreto* form. The largest works to date are freestanding works about 3m tall (unless you count the Hayward Gallery, which is, after all, an extremely big lump of concrete); the smallest is a few centimetres high and can be held in the palm of my hand.

David Batchelor, *Reef*, 2016. Plexiglass and concrete.

David Batchelor,
***Multi-Colour Chart 34*, 2018.**
Gloss paint on Dibond.

Colour Chart paintings

The *Concretos* relate closely to a long series of works on paper and paintings that I have been making since the late 1990s. The *Atomic* drawings (1997–) and the *Colour Chart* paintings (2010–2019) all employ the same basic device. In each drawing and painting, a colour-form is made from adhesive tape, liquid paint, spray paint, pastel or some combination of these materials. The addition of a rudimentary plinth or base gives the form above it a sense of weight, mass and balance. It becomes a sculptural fantasy: something that I never intended to build, even if I had the skills and resources, which I don't.

It was more than a decade after the first *Atomic* drawing that I began to make larger-scale paintings (gloss paint poured onto aluminium composite panels) and a little after that I made my first *Concreto* sculptures. The schematic base or plinth device has been very useful and very tolerant: it has given me a lot of space to experiment with colours and materials and to develop my work. But at the same time, it is also a bit dumb: an almost cartoonish device, something that stands for something rather than being something in itself. This is more obviously the case with the works on paper and paintings, perhaps. And this may be one reason why I moved into three dimensions: a concrete base is always a specific material presence in the world, something I am reminded of every time I try to move the works around the studio.

Only a few works I have made (until the last couple of years) have not employed the colour-form-and-neutral-support device. Almost all of these have been illuminated works of one kind or another, and there is a fairly simple reason for this. Non-illuminated colour will always have to negotiate its presence with other elements of a work – structure, support, materials, etc. The great advantage of using coloured light is it tends quite literally to put all these elements into the shade. It is, in its way, unbeatable: luminous colour is the crack cocaine of chromatic experience. But this kind of high comes at a price: the most vibrant and emphatic form of colour is also the most fragile: at the flick of a switch, it is gone and as if it was never there. The fiery pool reflecting in the asphalt is a melancholy pleasure, perhaps, one that leaves absolutely no trace of its brief and brilliant existence.

David Batchelor, 'Caçamba', 2012. Industrial skip, neon, outside Galeria Leme, São Paulo (building designed by Paulo Mendes de Rocha).

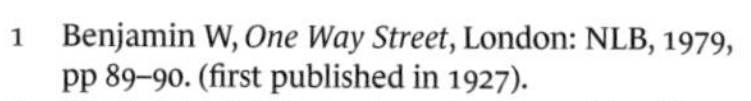

1 Benjamin W, *One Way Street*, London: NLB, 1979, pp 89–90. (first published in 1927).
2 Baudelaire C, 'The painter of modern life', 1863, in *Baudelaire: Selected Writings on Art and Artists*, Cambridge: Cambridge University Press, 1972, p 403.
3 See Batchelor D, *Concretos*, London: Anomie Press, 2022.

PROFILE

Colour as Activism

Guto Requena

Estudio Guto Requena, 'My Heart Beats Like Yours', 2018. Installation at Praça da República, São Paulo, Brazil.

Colour is a visual element that carries symbolic weight while adding different meaningful layers to those objects onto which it is applied. Our perceptions of colour are responsible for a series of conscious and unconscious stimuli that define our psychic-spatial relationship to the built environment. Therefore, its use can go beyond purely aesthetic definitions by connecting people with themselves, with others or with the spaces they are experiencing. Throughout my career as an architect, I seek to apply colour with an awareness of its transformative capacity, especially in urban-scale projects that have public visibility. It is in these spaces that we may impact more people and amplify the message we would like to convey.

My Heart Beats Like Yours

A project from 2018 entitled 'My Heart Beats Like Yours' taps into the power of empathy and design-as-activism to create a tribute to the LGBTQ+ community in Brazil. Located in São Paulo's iconic República square, the interactive design marks the site of the first meeting of the LGBTQ+ activist community in 1978. The diversity and inequities of Brazilian society are visible every day, as a stream of passers-by and the numerous homeless people gather in the area. A hybrid between urban furniture and sculpture, the large (16m-tall) structure consists of a cylindrical metal infrastructure painted in the colours of the LGBTQ+ flag, which spreads out from a vertical core and meanders on the ground to serve as public seating. The cylinders transmit audio statements by LGBTQ+ activists that recount their experiences and are overlaid with the sound of their heartbeats. These pulses inform an algorithm that models the pattern of the structure's night-time lighting, while the stories are repeated in an uninterrupted 24-hour loop.

#TogetherWithPride (#JuntosComOrgulho)

Another work, '#TogetherWithPride', comprises an intervention on a building facade located in an iconic address in São Paulo, which is painted with the colours of the LGBTQ+ movement to commemorate Pride month. Facebook promoted a live event that featured prominent names in Brazilian music and invited the participants to contribute to the moment by sharing their stories using the hashtag #JuntosComOrgulho (#TogetherWithPride). Through the deployment of software connected to the Facebook app, the number of comments sent by the public were counted and displayed in real-time via a special instrument we nicknamed the 'Pridemeter'. When the number of comments reached 100% on the 'Pridemeter', the system discharged the first two colours of the flag in a cascading chromatic band of pigment.

Estudio Guto Requena, Coloured facade of '#TogetherWithPride' (#JuntosComOrgulho), Minhocão, 2021.

Estudio Guto Requena, '#TogetherWithPride' (#JuntosComOrgulho), Minhocão, 2021. When the 'Pridemeter' reaches 100%, the second band of colour is painted on the facade.

'#JuntosComOrgulho' manifests a symbolic landmark in the city by making visible the voices of this community on a 40m-high facade. The wider area, Elevado João Goulart ('Minhocão'), is currently in the process of transforming into an urban park and open-air art gallery: approximately 30 murals by different artists, alongside several spontaneous projections, are on display – a number that has increased significantly in the last year.

These two projects illustrate instances where specific colours associated with the flag of a community served as the starting point for design thinking and its application.

Over the last 10 years at Estudio Guto Requena, technology has been an ally in our quest to reflect on possible futures that foreground empathy and connection. Our application of biofeedback sensors captures users' biological data (heartbeats, neural waves, among others) or data from the environment and translates them into interactive visual graphics. This is one of the main research fields of the practice, and requires the involvement of multidisciplinary teams in the design process: architects, but also computer scientists, designers, visual artists and psychologists. It consists of choosing subjective (emotions) or objective (temperature, movement) data and developing an interpretation of numerical data in shapes and designs.

One of the possibilities is to use colour as a tool to translate emotions: red may represent a more energetic, tense person with accelerated heartbeats, while a shade of blue can express calmer emotions.

Estudio Guto Requena, 'Light Creature' at night, São Paulo, 2015.

Light Creature

A hotel facade design entitled 'Light Creature' was executed on one of the busiest avenues in São Paulo and entails signage for passers-by according to the environmental conditions of its surroundings. During daylight hours, a coat of sheet metal creates a pixelated skin in blue, grey and gold. This urban camouflage was conceived from the analysis of on-site ambient noise by pairing parametric scripting with colourful graphic patterns based on a 24-hour soundscape captured at various points around the hotel's third floor. A digital model of the building generated the peaks and valleys of the audio file four times, representing the four periods of the day: morning, afternoon, evening and night. With the help of the Grasshopper app, the various sound volumes control the position of each metal panel. Peak audio levels define the position of the gold sheet, moderate levels define the navy blue, quiet levels define the light blue and silence defines the grey.

At night, the metal skin is lit with 200 strips of low-energy LED lighting that give life to the luminous creature and create an interactive dynamic with the city and its inhabitants. This creature behaves on its own, reacting in real-time to environmental stimuli and people. Ambient noise directly affects the creature's form and motion via microphones installed on the building. Local air quality changes its colours through another group of sensors. Polluted air gives the creature warmer tones such as reds and oranges. When air quality improves, cooler colours, such as blues and greens, appear. Once again, a mobile app allows the public to engage directly in two ways: through touch (via a visual dynamic inspired by the classic 'Game of Life', developed in the 1970s by the English mathematician John Horton Conway) and through voice by speaking with the building, which in turn registers sound waves on its facade. We hacked the building by plugging in sensors, chips, microcontrollers and LED strips to make it communicative; the facade responds to stimuli from its surroundings and invites the population of São Paulo to consider its own behaviour. Sound and air quality provide key data points that index the quality of urban landscapes in large cities.

Estudio Guto Requena, 'Dancing Pavilion', Rio de Janeiro, 2016.

Estudio Guto Requena, 'Dancing Pavilion', Rio de Janeiro, 2016. Facade detail.

Dancing Pavilion

Created for the 2016 Rio de Janeiro Olympics, the 'Dancing Pavilion' approaches the application of colour in a similar manner to the 'Light Creature' project. Each base module of the facade is identified by a colour, thereby creating a pixelated effect that connects a digital aesthetic to the physical universe. In this case, the choice of palette represents diversity. Together, the modules formed a kinetic skin with around 500 discs that had coloured and mirrored faces moving in sync, all the while visualising the passage of light and changing colours. This mirrored skin spins, opening and closing as it creates optical effects. Scattered sensors inside the dance floor also stimulate the skin, via the beat of the music or the excited commotion of moving bodies. Under direct sunlight, the kinetic pavilion creates graphics of light and shadow on the floor and its surroundings. At night, light cannons dramatically cast explosive beams outside, calling attention to points as far as the entrance of the Olympic Park. It is an emotional architecture that shivers like an excited body. In this marriage of design and technology, we wanted to provoke a worldwide audience; we wanted to take them from an everyday world to a dream state of joy and escapism.

CASE STUDY

Colouring the Public Realm

Javier González Rivero

100architects, 'The Nest', Chengdu, 2021–. Aerial view.

Urban playgrounds

In our daily praxis at 100architects, we constantly search for new ways to improve our cities and the experience of their citizens, in particular their interactions within the public realm. The office was born with this mission in mind and driven by a passion for shaping friendlier urban landscapes. Our work aims to transform cityscapes as we know them today into the hyperstimulating ones we envision for tomorrow. In pursuit of this aim, we deploy colour as a primary design tool to transform urban environments. Utilising vibrant colour in unexpected and surprising ways is key to our success in creating memorable civic experiences. The projects discussed here serve as case studies and one strand of our output: spaces for and about play.

100architects, 'The Nest', Chengdu, 2021–. Little chicks and their mother bird in their nest.

The Nest

Beyond the many advantages of living in the city, significant drawbacks persist. Urban residents must often contend with the mental health and quality of life challenges that are also associated with high-density environments. It is our contention that public spaces have undergone very little innovation in the last 100 years. This is not to say that urban plazas, squares and the like haven't adapted and responded in sophisticated ways to current trends and available technology.

However, new generations of urban residents seek unique experiences, and prefer investing in memorable living scenarios rather than in owning products. They have come to expect varying sensory stimulations and, in that regard, our urban playscapes have the potential to offer new forms of recreation to meet the increased demand for urban stimulation and fantasy.[1]

'The Nest', for instance, is a perfect example of this new generation of public spaces. New Hope Group asked us to renovate and beautify their community plaza, located in Chengdu, the capital of the Chinese province of Sichuan, with only one proviso: that we incorporate their IP image, the Bird.

Our response was to create a whole narrative driven by the idea of a magical moment of birth of two little chicks in their nest, accompanied by their mother bird, hence the name of the project: 'The Nest'.

Viewed as an 'urban toy for the city', the project reflects the studio's belief that play is not only for kids. We designed this urban playscape to boost joy and entertainment for kids and adults alike, regardless of their age. A colourful playscape can act as an urban attractor and catalyser of social interactions, calling attention to itself by standing out from its surrounding environment.

100architects, 'The Nest', Chengdu, 2021–. Round ping-pong table, for youngsters and adults within the urban playground.

100architects, 'The Nest', Chengdu, 2021–. Night effect highlighting the most significant aesthetical attributes of the project.

100architects, 'Lollipop Street', Shanghai, 2022–. A public space that sparks joy and happiness.

In addition to the creation of green spaces, active spaces and safe zones in the city,[2] some studies show that colour can also influence our mental and physical wellbeing.[3] Research has shown that colour has a significant impact on the environmental qualities and conditions of contemporary urban environments, and, by extension, a big impact on human use and perception. Since we are social animals, both our perceptions and experience of public spaces are decisive for our wellbeing; the public realm is a playground. The implementation of colour in the public space can certainly become a powerful tool in this regard, and significant for the welfare of its citizens.

All our projects have this particular approach to colour, as the main striking point during the day. However, projects are also used during the night, when the perception of colour is not as vivid. The night effect of the project not only provides a sense of safety to the space, but also turns the diurnal colourful experience into a whimsical nocturnal one, enhancing the most significant features of the project, such as the meandering shapes of all the eggshells through decorative perimeter lighting.

Lollipop Street

'Lollipop Street' is another public space activation project. Aimed at creating an outdoor play area as a welcoming gathering point for the community by a splash of contrasting colour, its siting is at the front plaza of Jinyang L-Site Mall, in Shanghai's Free Trade Zone of Lujiazui, in Pudong District.

It is a project inspired by an imaginary 'candy world', borrowing shapes and colours from pop culture objects such as candy canes, lollipops and popsicles. It depicts an eye-catching, colourful and intricate knot, designed as an eventful, tangled path; by twisting, bending and entangling, we created pockets of opportunity for play, entertainment and leisure.

Well-designed public spaces are known to impact positively on the health and wellbeing of citizens, thanks to attributes such as openness, accessibility, walkability, free mobility, playability, shareability, social connectivity, etc. In addition, vivid and contrasting colours, when strategically used, can also provide welfare by inspiring joy and happiness to citizens, by immersing them in remarkable and iconic environments like 'Lollipop Street'.

Above: 100architects, 'Lollipop Street', Shanghai, 2022–. Aerial view of 'Lollipop Street' and its intricate knot.

Right: 100architects, 'Lollipop Street', Shanghai, 2022–. Happy colours contrasting with the background.

100architects, 'Creek Play', Dubai, 2019–. Arabesque capsule designed as a vertical maze.

Creek Play

Commissioned by Emaar Properties, Creek Play is dedicated to enhancing the public realm of their latest ambitious project: Dubai Creek Harbour, a pedestrian-friendly new hotspot in the city of Dubai. 100architects designed a stimulating permanent intervention for entertainment along 350m of waterfront promenade at Creek Island's Marina.

Conceptually conceived as a playful village inspired by Dubai's vernacular arabesque shapes used in traditional doors and windows, the proposal adds a pinch of colour and playfulness along the meandering promenade and is split into seven focal nodes of activity, evenly distributed along the promenade's entire length. The seven zones have a symbolic meaning related to the seven emirates that make up the United Arab Emirates.

Each node comprises a conglomeration of capsules forming a stimulating village of fun, in which each capsule offers a different function, such as sitting, swinging, sliding, climbing, lying down, playing, hanging, etc., all of which encourage social interactions.

We strongly believe that hyperstimulating public spaces have the power to produce new dynamics and opportunities for flourishing neighbourhoods. In a world where technology, social media and online retail are replacing our natural meeting places and our traditional ways of socialising, applying vivid colours to our collective spaces gives us the opportunity to explore ways to momentarily detach people from their screens by first capturing their attention and then – through our designs – encouraging everyday human interactions in the urban sphere. Ultimately, real-life connectivity is the kind of kinship that triggers productivity and innovation.

100architects, 'Creek Play', Dubai, 2019–. Capsules inspired by vernacular arabesque architecture.

100architects, 'Creek Play', Dubai, 2019–. Playful node encouraging social interaction.

1 100architects Manifesto, https://100architects.com/manifesto (accessed 7 February 2023).
2 Centre for Urban Design and Mental Health, 'How urban design can impact mental health', https://www.urbandesignmentalhealth.com/how-urban-design-can-impact-mental-health.html (accessed 7 February 2023).
3 Mahnke FH 'Color in architecture – more than just decoration', *Archinect*, 20 July 2012, https://archinect.com/features/article/53292622/color-in-architecture-more-than-just-decoration (accessed 25 June 2019).

CASE STUDY

'What Black is This, You Say?'

A Conversation between Amanda Williams and Jasmine Benyamin

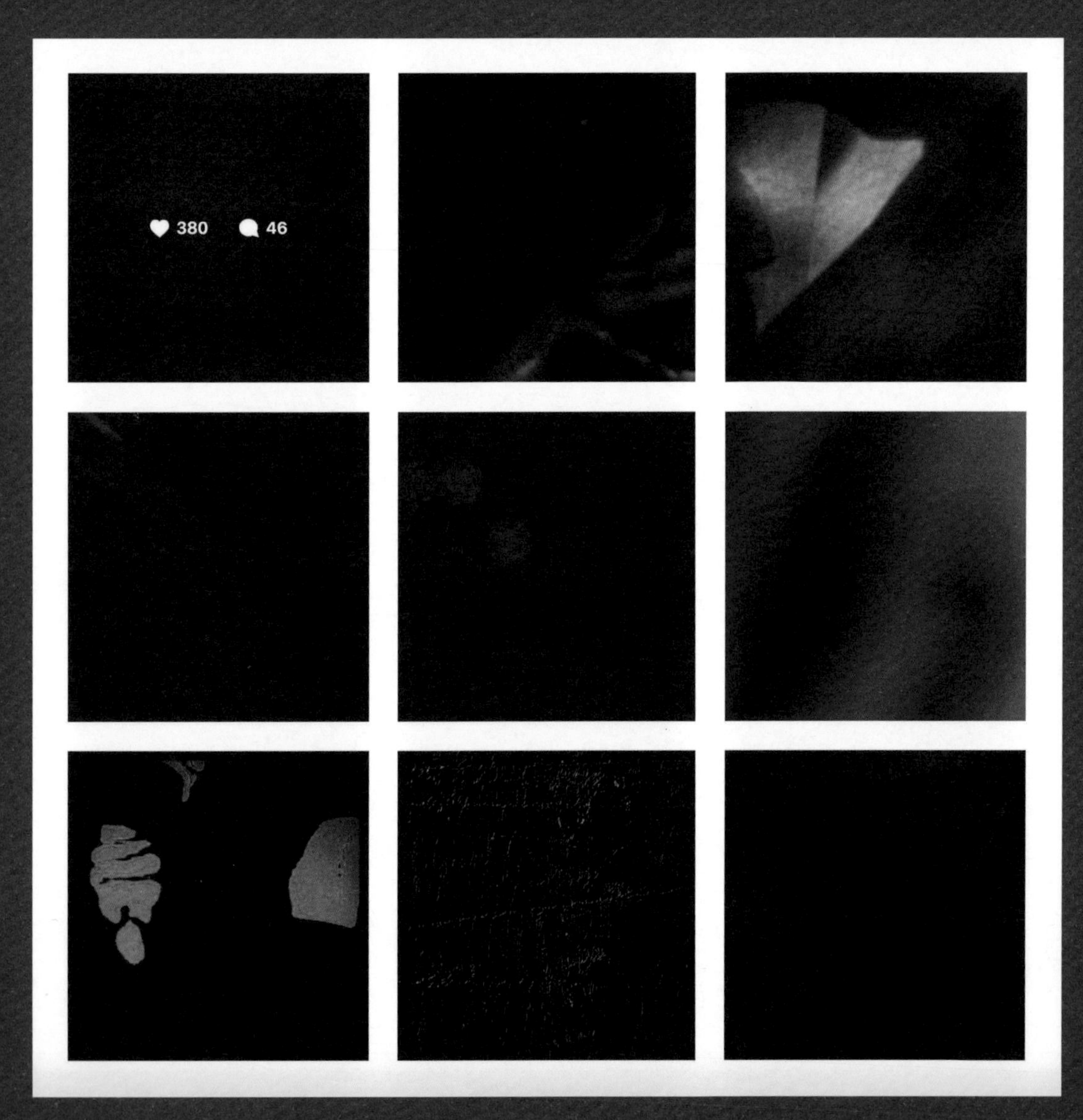

A 'Grid of Squares' from Amanda Williams' Instagram account, 2020.

In what by now has become a quote readily attributed to Amanda Williams, she notes, 'Colour is everything to me. You can't just say "black". Which one?'

The ongoing series 'What Black is This, You Say?' does not neatly fit the mould of an architectural 'case study'. When asked if she considers herself a multihyphenate (artist-architect), Williams smiles: 'I oscillate on how I answer these sorts of questions. There is always a spatial element in the work, be it painting or building. [It] is architectural, but not in the traditional sense, so I don't describe it like that anymore.'

A pause and then she adds: 'But anybody that is an architect can see the spatial concerns.'

Williams' refusal to put her work in a disciplinary box reflects an evolution from her institutional upbringing (she has a degree in architecture from Cornell University with an emphasis in fine arts) as well as her interest in creating conversations across disciplines and audiences.

There are many throughlines in the 'What Black is This, You Say?' series – concerns that span her production, with some more obvious than others. At all scales and media, context is central; whether through Instagram, on derelict houses in the south side of Chicago or in a gallery setting, Williams is 'invested and engaged in the spaces in which the work finds itself referencing'. With context comes colour; whether as material exploration, as social commentary or as full-scale application, her use of it is unapologetically opinionated: 'Living in, and coming from, Chicago makes thinking about colour as a neutral element impossible. Racism is so entrenched in that city's hues, and therefore my thinking around colour is always couched within race. It takes a tremendous amount of effort to think about it beyond or outside of race.'

Instagram blackout

The first iteration of the project appeared as digital content: a lengthy series of posts on Instagram (a remote site of enquiry during the global pandemic), spurred on by #BlackoutTuesday. While nearly all the responses posted that day were of black square monoliths, Williams leveraged her knowledge of colour as well as her social media platform to engage many shades of blackness. In so doing, she made her ambivalence clear. Which black?

'When I did the Instagram posts, I had no intention of turning them into paintings. I was just stuck at home and mad,' she notes.

Scrolling through her feed, the resonance of the tonal planes is amplified with the textual supplement: operating as titles or extended captions, this particular mode of writing simultaneously describes and performs Williams' message.

Amanda Williams, 'What Black is This, You Say?', Storefront for Art and Architecture, New York, 2020–2021.

Amanda Williams, 'What Black is This, You Say?', Storefront for Art and Architecture, New York, 2020–2021.

Storefront for Art and Architecture

Exploring the physical and perceptual modalities of 'What Black is this, You Say?' seemed inevitable, and in June 2020 Williams was invited by the Storefront for Art and Architecture in New York to develop a public version of the app-initiated project by intervening on the unique tectonics of the facade.

Taking advantage of the jump in scale and given the partial lifting of pandemic restrictions, Williams began by hosting a series of painting sessions. Debuting a year later, 12 of the roughly 150 shades used in 2020 were brought back, and captions were superimposed on the rotating panels. In this new urban context, the twin functions of the Instagram captions (description and performance) held firm. The texture of the existing envelope combined with the new chromatic skin of varying blacks provided a literal and experiential heft to the project.

Amanda Williams, 'What Black is This, You Say?', Storefront for Art and Architecture, New York, 2020–2021.

Amanda Williams, *CandyLadyBlack (Located somewhere between when Millie Cox finally met Florida Evans)*, 2022.

Gagosian Gallery

Williams revisited the domestic scale of the Storefront project in the most recent iteration of the series, at the Gagosian Gallery (Park and 75, New York City). In this case, the interiors that were recalled referred to the ubiquitous Candy Lady – a black female entrepreneur, 'a woman working from her home... but from a completely different economic model'. Williams returned to the series' Instagram origins by resuming work at the square aspect ratio of the app. She explains, 'Photos [from the Instagram posts] became the baseline for the sketches in watercolour, which scaled up to 20 x 20 inch and then eventually to 60 x 60 inch.'

The compositional structure of the paintings invites us to touch, to smell, to consume; they look good enough to eat, and that is partly the point. The over-saturated canvases don't index anything 'real'. On the contrary, they reference the processed and artificial qualities of the sugary treats that were handed out to kids in the neighbourhood.

These canvases are topographies of sorts, with zones of relative safety and hazard left to the eye of the beholder. Surfaces that migrate from high gloss to flat, thick and thin take on distinct sheens. 'The luminescence is what brings the paintings back to architecture,' Williams explains.

Nonetheless, it is clear that this work has garnered larger audiences. 'Having them in the gallery creates an even bigger dialog,' says Williams.

Indeed, the series takes us on a cartographic journey – one that expands our definitions of what mapping should look like. Not relying on readymade colour wheels, Williams' hues index chromatic paths across uncharted territories – landscapes that tell the story of race in America. Can colour be materially opaque yet conceptually transparent? She has her own ideas about the project, but the artefacts also operate as placeholders for future readings, and, as such, are never complete. Asked if the project proposes any remedies, Williams' reply is emphatic: 'There are no solutions posited here. The work is about joy. And this community has a right to joy.'[1]

1. Williams A, in conversation with Benyamin J, 10 June 2022.

Right: Amanda Williams, *CandyLadyBlack (The Champagne is Burned)*, 2022.

Below: Amanda Williams, *CandyLadyBlack (wine candy grape nowalater sneak)*, 2022.

Adam Wiseman's Film Ends series is the result of photographic lab processes not composition. Unexposed celluloid from negatives Wiseman scanned for his forthcoming book, *Elvis Never Was in Acapulco*, was chemically developed, inadvertently producing atmospheric, technicolored images.

Final Word

Uncolour

Mimi Zeiger

Blues

Sheila Heti, in her 2022 novel *Pure Colour,* describes the room of her protagonist's dying father. Taped to the wall is a green towel used to block out sunlight. A deep yellow candle sits on a black-and-white plate. On the floor by her father's bed: a pink towel. Or was it? 'It was green,' she writes. 'Colours matter. Colours can be hard to remember.'[1]

Colour commands our senses, our spatial awareness, our emotions, but as Heti's short sentences point out, colour is changeable, making it difficult to recall. Any purity we might have come to expect slips out of grasp over time. Neuroscience research supports this instability between colour and memory. A paper in the *Journal of Experimental Psychology: General* notes that our brains store colour in broad categories by hue.[2] Blue, for example, is the very best version of blue; Facebook blue, Le Corbusier blue, sky blue, Yves Klein blue all fall under the most generic heading and our memories must labour past the archetypical to find a precise shade of cobalt or navy.

'We tag the colour with a coarse label. That then makes our memories more biased, but still pretty useful,' cognitive psychologist Jonathan Flombaum told *Neuroscience News*.[3] Our memories, like history, are clouded by biases and tastes.

1 Heti S, *Pure Colour: A Novel*, UK: Farrar, Straus and Giroux, 2022, p 23; excerpt in *Granta* as 'Pure Colour', *Granta* 158, 10 February 2022, https://granta.com/pure-colour-sheila-heti (accessed 14 February 2023).
2 Bae G, Olkkonen M, Allred S, Flombaum J, 'Why some colours appear more memorable than others: A model combining categories and particulars in colour working memory', *Journal of Experimental Psychology: General*, 2015, p 144.
3 Rosen J, 'Why it's hard to remember colours', *Neuroscience News*, 2 June 2015, https://neurosciencenews.com/visual-working-memory-color-2083 (accessed 14 February 2023).
4 https://hyperallergic.com/253361/art-historian-finds-racist-joke-hidden-under-malevichs-black-square (accessed 14 February 2023). The artist had scrawled, 'Battle of negroes in a dark cave', supposedly in dialogue with the early modernist monochromatic artwork by French writer and humorist Alphonse Allais, *Combat de Nègres dans une cave pendant la nuit* (1897).
5 Heti S, *Pure Colour*, p 24.
6 Pantone.com, 'Introducing PANTONE® 17-3938 Very Peri: Pantone Color of the Year 2022', https://www.pantone.com/articles/press-releases/introducing-pantone-17-3938-very-peri-pantone-color-of-the-year-2022 (accessed 14 February 2023).
7 https://www.pantone.com/color-of-the-year-2023 (accessed 14 February 2023).

Blacks

In the slippage between matter and memory is a place where meaning shifts from definite to flickering, like the candle in the dying father's room. What if we call this indeterminate space 'uncolour'? For its mutability, its condition of having become unmoored, not because it has no colour or is colour blind. Neutrals are not neutral. Beiges, tans and creams – those slightly muddy shades so indicative of a particular type of benign interiority that they seem designed to be forgotten in a haze of hotel lobbies and ladies' restrooms. White, that plain coat of Ripolin that Carolyn Kane in 'Arch-White' argues is the moral primer of modern whiteness. But white yellows under fluorescent light, greys under smoggy skies. Its aesthetic is compromised, undermined by daily existence. Its innocence is a false memory better forgotten.

Black, like white, is absolute totality and negation of colour. And yet, within its tonal variations, absolutism gives way to the browns, greys and blues embodied in earth, ash and skin – even as our brain succumbs to bias in remembering black and white with little nuance. Which is why the question posed by Amanda Williams – 'What Black is This, You Say?' – resonates so profoundly. Her query and subsequent Instagram posts and installation taunt a media culture of corrective universalism. The singularity of a black square attempts to placate histories upon histories of racial violence and bias, but in doing so mutes joys of infinite varieties of blackness, and the sorrows of colourism.

Indeed, no black square is unequivocally black. There's the story of when curators and researchers at Russia's State Tretyakov Gallery used new imaging technology to reveal the layers hidden under the cracking paint of one of three versions of Kazimir Malevich's *The Black Square* (1915); they found not only a proto-Supremacist composition, but also a handwritten reference to a nasty racist joke.[4] This repulsive reflection of black-on-black shifts us into the realm of 'uncolour', where the art historical understanding we might ascribe to *The Black Square* is detonated. Shrapnel of meaning is all that remains. What black is this, you say? It is a black of more dubious origin than ever remembered.

Violets

Heti casts the remembrance of the dying father's room in a gauze of 'maroonish light', writing, 'Colour is not just a representation of the world, but of the feelings in a room, and the meaningfulness of a room in time.'[5] Umbral in her description, she binds colour to temporality, thus linking two elusive characters to each other, both warm and oozing like the oils in a lava lamp.

In 2022, Pantone named Very Peri (Pantone 17-3938) the colour of the year. It's a violaceous shade between blue and lilac destined to be forgotten. Leatrice Eiseman, executive director at the Pantone Color Institute, remarked that the hue carries a spritely attitude and creative expression, however she couches her remarks (made at the end of 2021) with the sentence, 'As we move into a world of unprecedented change, the selection of PANTONE 17-3938 Very Peri brings a novel perspective and vision of the trusted and beloved blue colour family.'[6] Like Heti, she cannot help but slip into an uncoloured mood and connect Very Peri to the many difficulties and ambiguities of our time.

Viva Magenta, the colour of 2023, was announced at Art Basel Miami with great fanfare and evocations of the digital and game cultures: 'Welcome to the Magentaverse,' reads the website. It's a 'boundaryless shade that is manifesting as a standout statement', gushed Eiseman.[7] But digital colours, as Galo Canizares reminds us in his 'semi-technical reflection', are perceptually volatile, upending expectations and producing effects. Chroma key green and blue, for example, are eye-catching fluorescent 'uncolours' designed to be seen by the nonhuman eye, then replaced or forgotten.

Louisa Hutton evokes Josef Albers' notion of *Farbraum* (illusionary coloured space) in describing how Sauerbruch Hutton's use of colour aims to achieve a condition that alternates between two- and three-dimensional space – a spatial analogue to the optical tricks of Albers' colour theories. If architecture and colour is an oscillation between the visual and the corporeal, as Hutton suggests, then 'uncolour' exists in this flicker, but is a different zoetrope – a fleeting illusion of meaning across ambiguous time.

About the Contributors

Maya Alam is an architect, artist and designer. She is a founding partner of A/P Practice and currently holds the chair 'Theory and Discourse of Design' at the Bergische Universität Wuppertal. Alam was the inaugural recipient of the Boghosian Fellowship, the Dekoloniale Berlin Residency and the Schloss Solitude Fellowship. Her work negotiates ideas of multivalent identities, and she utilises imaging technologies to explore forms of engagement that allow for more than one viewpoint.

David Batchelor is an artist and writer based in London. He has exhibited internationally for over three decades and has published a number of books on colour, including *Chromophobia* (Reaktion Books, 2000).

fala is an architecture practice based in Porto, founded in 2013, led by Filipe Magalhães, Ana Luisa Soares, Ahmed Belkhodja and Lera Samovich.

Galo Canizares is a designer, writer and educator currently researching the sociotechnical networks of relations between design's softwarisation and the architectural imagination. He is the author of *Digital Fabrications: Designer Stories for a Software-Based Planet* (Applied Research and Design, 2019), a collection of essays on software and design. He is an assistant professor of architecture at the University of Kentucky College of Design.

Courtney Coffman is Manager of Lectures and Publications at Princeton University's School of Architecture. She has served as a content and copy editor for various architectural publications and monographs. Her own writings explore the visual culture and relational aesthetics of contemporary architecture and design, alongside alternative histories and popular taste.

Marcelyn Gow is a partner at servo los angeles, a design collaborative focused on the intersection of architectural ecologies and material practices that engage multiple environmental histories and possible futures. Gow is an Undergraduate Programs Chair, and design, history-theory faculty at SCI-Arc, where she also teaches in the postgraduate Design Theory and Pedagogy program. Gow's doctoral dissertation *Invisible Environment: Art, Architecture and a Systems Aesthetic* explores the relationship between aesthetic research and technological innovation in the context of collaborative practices.

Louisa Hutton is an architect and founding partner of Sauerbruch Hutton. She has taught at the Architectural Association and was a visiting professor at Harvard's GSD. Hutton was a commissioner at CABE as well as a member of the first steering committee for the Bundesstiftung Baukultur. Lecturing and participating in juries worldwide, Hutton is an Honorary Fellow of the American Institute of Architects and a Royal Academician of Arts. She was awarded an OBE in 2015.

Sam Jacob is principal of Sam Jacob Studio for architecture and design, a practice whose work spans scales and disciplines including architecture, design and exhibition projects. Recent work includes a new building in London's Hoxton, and projects for the Science Museum, the V&A and Somerset House. He is a professor of architecture at the University of Illinois at Chicago and is currently visiting professor at TU Wien. He is author of *Make It Real, Architecture as Enactment* (Strelka Press, 2014). Previously, he was a founding director of FAT Architecture.

Carolyn L Kane is the author of *Electrographic Architecture: New York Color, Las Vegas Light*, and America's White Imaginary (University of California Press, 2023); *High-Tech Trash: Glitch Noise and Aesthetic Failure* (University of California Press, 2019); and *Chromatic Algorithms: Synthetic Colour, Computer Art, and Aesthetics after Code* (University of Chicago Press, 2014).

Guto Requena is a Brazilian architect with a strong academic vein and for nine years he was a researcher at Nomads.Usp, Center for the Study of Interactive Dwellings at the University of São Paulo. He is now a professor at the Université Sorbonne in Paris. Since 2013, Requena has been delivering lectures and workshops around the world. In 2019, he published the book *Habitar Híbrido* by Editora Senac. Estudio Guto Requena is a multidisciplinary creative studio founded by Requena and based in São Paulo, investigating the intersections among architecture, product design, communication and technology, and exploring new forms of design and digital technologies that can stimulate emotions, empathy and the sense of collectiveness. The practice's projects hybridise the analogical with the virtual.

Javier González Rivero is a Spanish architect with more than 15 years of international working experience. He holds a Master's Degree in Advanced Architecture from the Institute for Advanced Architecture of Catalonia, Barcelona. He is one of the Managing Partners at 100architects, a pioneering firm based in Shanghai, which was born with the mission of improving the public realm in cities, and the experiences of their citizens.

Paulette Singley is a professor of architecture at Woodbury University, in Burbank, California. She served as the Adele Chatfield-Taylor Rome Prize fellow at the American Academy in Rome during spring of 2021, authored *How to Read Architecture: An Introduction to Interpreting the Built Environment* (Routledge, 2019), co-edited *Eating Architecture* (MIT Press, 2006) and co-edited *Architecture: In Fashion* (Princeton Architectural Press, 1994).

Amanda Williams is a visual artist who trained as an architect. Her creative practice employs colour as an operative means for drawing attention to the complex ways race informs how we assign value to the spaces we occupy. Her ongoing series, 'What Black is This, You Say?', is a multiplatform project that explores the wide range of meanings and conceptual colours that connote blackness. Williams' installations, sculptures, paintings and works on paper seek to inspire new ways of looking at the familiar and, in the process, raise questions about the state of urban space and ownership in America.

Mimi Zeiger is a Los Angeles-based critic, editor and curator. She was co-curator of the US Pavilion for the 2018 Venice Architecture Biennale and the 2020–2021 cycle of Exhibit Columbus. Zeiger is visiting faculty at the Southern California Institute of Architecture.

Recommended Reading

Books

Albers J, *Interaction of Colour – 50th Anniversary Edition*, Yale University Press, 2013.

Andreoli E and D'Andrea L, *La Arquitectura de Freddy Mamani Silvestre*, Artes Gráficas Sagitario SRL, 2014.

Bailkin J, 'Indian Yellow: Making and Breaking the Imperial Palette', in Jay M and Ramaswamy S (eds), *Empires of Vision*, Duke University Press, 2014.

Batchelor D, *The Luminous and the Grey*, Reaktion Books, 2014.

Batchelor D, *Chromophobia*, Reaktion Books, 2000.

Hutton L, *Sauerbruch Hutton – Colour in Architecture*, Distanz, 2012.

Kane CL, *Electrographic Architecture: New York Color, Las Vegas Light, and America's White Imaginary*, University of California Press, 2023.

Léger F, 'Problèmes de la Couleur', 1954, in *Functions of Painting*, Viking Press, 1973.

Lepik A, Zweite A and Burmester A, *Sauerbruch Hutton Architects: Museum Brandhorst: The Architecture*, Hatje Cantz, 2009.

Maas W et al., *Green Dream: How Future Cities Can Outsmart Nature*, NAi, 2010.

Manferdini E (ed), *Elena Manferdini*, monograph on Atelier Manferdini's work from 2004 to 2012, Equalbooks, 2013.

Manferdini E (ed), *Landscapes and Portraits*, two-volume monograph on Atelier Manferdini's work from 2013 to 2019, Beijing University of Technology, 2019.

Olds OM, *Trinity of Color, or, The Law of Chromatics, or, How to Paint*, University of Maryland, 1892.

Plant R, *The Pink Triangle: The Nazi War Against Homosexuals*, Henry Holt and Company, 1986.

Ruhi P (ed), *The Domain of Paint*, monograph on Atelier Manferdini's work, Kasra Publishing, 2022.

Sharpe C, *In the Wake: On Blackness and Being*, Duke University Press, 2016.

St Clair K, *The Secret Lives of Colour*, Penguin Books, 2017.

Teyssot G, *The American Lawn,* Princeton Architectural Press with Canadian Centre for Architecture, 1999.

Articles

Byrne D, 'Colours/Pink: Not so sweet afterall', *Cabinet Magazine* 11, 2003.

Covington E, 'Pinking Virgil: The B-side', *Damn Magazine* 76, 2020.

Garcia M, 'Racist in the machine: The disturbing implications of algorithmic bias', *World Policy Journal* 33(4), 2016.

Hammer I, 'White, everything white? Josef Frank's Villa Beer (1930) in Vienna and its materiality in the context of "white cubes"', *Built Heritage* 4(2), 2020.

Joblove GH and Greenberg D, 'Colour spaces for computer graphics', in SIGGRAPH '78: *Proceedings of the 5th Annual Conference on Computer Graphics and Interactive Techniques,* August 1978, pp 20–25.

Kittler FA, 'Computer graphics: A semi-technical introduction', *Grey Room* 2, Winter, 2001.

Koreitem Z, 'Some notes on making images with computers', e-flux Architecture, July 2019.

Manferdini E and Griggs C, 'Colour corrections', *Log* 49, Summer 2020, pp 105–109.

Puente M and Loureiro R, 'Fala Atelier (Porto)', *2G* 80, 2020.

Warburton A, 'RGBFAQ', 27'38" video essay, subtitled, 2020.

Wigley M, 'Chronic whiteness', e-flux Architecture, November 2020.

Image Credits

VI
Ola Kolehmainen
VII, 35, 38, 39, 40
Maya Alam
IX bottom, 23, 28
Galo Canizares
VIII, 17, 18
Florencia Blanco
IX top
Ayla Hibri
X, XII top
Rex Zou
XII bottom
Alessandra Chemollo
XIII bottom, 55, 57, 58, 59 bottom
Sam Jacob Studio
XIII top
Ricardo Loureiro
1
Creative Commons / Photo Sam Lambert
2, 5
Creative Commons / public domain
3 top and bottom
RIBA Collections, Bernard Hugh Cox
4, 6
Illustration courtesy of Fondation Le Corbusier (FLC/ADAGP)
8
RIBA Collections
11
Jerald Cooper @hoodmidcenturymodern
12
Ira Brian Miller @irabrianmiller
14, 20
Tatewaki Nio
15
Markus Wilthaner
16
Andrew Kovacs
24 top, 24 middle
(ab)Normal
24 bottom
Office CA
26 top, 67, 69 top, 73 bottom, 74
Wikimedia Commons
26 bottom left, 26 bottom right
Paul Bourke
30, 31
NEMESTUDIO
32
MILLIØNS
37 top, middle, bottom
Ibiye Camp
41, 42
Folly Feast Lab
46, 47, 48, 49
Joshua White
50, 51, 52
Damjan Jovanovic
56, 57, 60 top, 61
Jim Stephenson
59 top
Rob Parish
60 bottom
Hedley Fruits
62, 63
Andy Mathews
64
Sarah Duncan
68
NASA/GSFC/METI/ERSDAC/JAROS, and U.S./Japan ASTER Science Team
69 bottom
Piet Niemann
70
Stefano Boeri Architetti
72, 73 top
New-Territories / R&Sie(n) / f.Roche
76
Sebastian Donath / Sauerbruch Hutton
77 top, bottom, 80, 83 top, 85 top
Sauerbruch Hutton
78
Hélène Binet
79 top
Charles Stebbings
79 bottom
Bitter+Bredt
81 top right, bottom
Jan Bitter
82
Andreas Lechtape
84, 85 bottom
Annette Kisling
83 bottom
Noshe
86, 87 top, bottom, 88
fala
89 top, 89 bottom, 90, 91
Francisco Ascensão
92
Ivo Tavares
95, 97
Victor Frankowski
98, 100
Lucy Dawkins
99
FXP Photography
101
David Batchelor
102
Ana Mello
104, 105 top
Manuel Sá
105 bottom
André Klotz
106, 107
Fernanda Ligabue, Rafael Frazão
108, 109 top, bottom, 110 top, bottom, 111 top, bottom
100 Architects / Photo: Rex Zou
112, 113 top, bottom
Amey Kandalgaonkar
114
Amanda Williams Instagram / public access
116 top, bottom, 117
Amanda Williams LLC / Photography by Michael Oliver
118, 119 top, bottom
Amanda Williams LLC / Photography by Jacob Hand
120
Adam Wiseman

Index

Index

Index